Contents

4 · Contents

YORK NOTES

General Editors: Professor A.N. Jeffares (*University of Stirling*) & Professor Suheil Bushrui (*American University of Beirut*)

YORK PRESS
Immeuble Esseily, Place Riad Solh, Beirut.

LONGMAN GROUP LIMITED
Longman House, Burnt Mill,
Harlow, Essex CM20 2JE, England
and Associated companies throughout the world

First published 1980
Second impression 1984
ISBN 0 582 78090 X
Printed in Hong Kong by
Sing Cheong Printing Co Ltd

Part 1

Introduction

SHAW'S REPUTATION as a dramatist is secure. His plays are performed more often than those of any other dramatist who writes or has written in English except for Shakespeare; indeed, again except for Shakespeare, Shaw is the best-known English dramatist in non-English-speaking countries.

1856 to 1881

George Bernard Shaw was born in Dublin, Ireland on 26 July 1856. His parents were Anglo-Irish Protestants, descended from good families. His father, a wholesale grain merchant, was the second cousin of a baronet; his mother was the daughter of a country gentleman. Although his family was snobbish about its social standing, and thought itself part of the gentry, his parents were poor. Shaw did not have an ordinary family life. His father was a hypocrite who warned against the dangers of drinking alcohol although he himself was a secret alcoholic; his best quality was a sense of humour. Shaw's mother was talented and kind, but she gave little attention to her two daughters and son. She was cold and reserved; music was her only passion. She spent her time pursuing a career as a singer. Disappointed with her husband she moved when Shaw was seventeen to London, where she supported herself as a music teacher.

Although taken to church and Sunday school regularly, Shaw later said that the family atmosphere was one of derisive free-thinking; he early lost his belief in Christianity. He grew up with music, painting and drama, but had little formal education. He was largely self-educated through reading and discussion. Throughout his life he had a contempt for schooling. He left school at the age of fifteen and during the next five years worked for a Dublin estate agent. He did well at business and was promoted rapidly, but he disliked office work and at the age of twenty (1876) left to go to London.

In London Shaw worked briefly for a telephone company and then decided to give up such work as against his 'nature', to be able to dedicate himself to a career as a writer. For the next twenty-two years he lived with his mother while he explored London's intellectual life and tried to make his way as a writer. He began with novels. He regularly wrote five pages a day for five years; the result was five novels which were rejected by book publishers, although four were serialised in small magazines during the period 1884–8.

1881 to 1885

During the early 1880s Shaw joined various intellectual debating societies which were then popular and influential in London. He became a lifelong vegetarian in 1881. In 1882 he was converted to socialism after attending a lecture by Henry George, the author of *Progress and Poverty*. In the same year he read the French translation of Karl Marx's *Das Kapital* (no English translation was then available) and in 1884 he joined the newly-founded Fabian Society; he was elected to the executive in 1885. Although the early Fabians were Marxists believing in revolution, Shaw and his two friends, Beatrice and Sidney Webb, converted the society to working through established political channels towards democratic socialism. While Shaw was not against revolutionary violence, he was aware that the Paris Commune of 1871 had failed to establish a communist government; lacking administrative knowledge and experience, it expired in violence. He thought that socialism must be prepared for by education, propaganda, and a knowledge of how government operates.

1885 to 1891

During the period 1885 to 1894 Shaw became well known in London as a writer for various newspapers and journals. He now earned enough as an author to be financially independent. He was book reviewer for the *Pall Mall Gazette* (1885–8), art critic for *The World* (1886–7), and music critic for *The Star* (1888–90). He played an important part in London's literary and intellectual life, editing, and contributing to, the *Fabian Essays in Socialism* (1889) and writing *The Quintessence of Ibsenism* (1891), which began as a talk before the Fabian Society. It is the first book in English on Ibsen and shows the influence of the Norwegian playwright Henrik Ibsen (1828–1906) on Shaw and the modern theatre.

In 1891 the Independent Theatre, dedicated to revitalising English drama, performed Ibsen's *Ghosts*. Five years earlier Shaw and a daughter of Karl Marx acted in a private performance of Ibsen's *A Doll's House*. The closeness felt between Ibsen's plays and social reform at the time can be seen by the fact that Marx's daughter translated Ibsen's plays into English during 1888–9.

The Quintessence of Ibsenism

Ibsen changed the direction of modern drama by introducing realistic social problems and by the discussion of formerly forbidden topics in his plays. *The Quintessence of Ibsenism* asks why one section of English society considers Ibsen the greatest living dramatist, while others consider him indecent and disgusting. Shaw claims that as civilisation changes, it is necessary to modify social institutions. Such social institutions as the family are conventions which civilisation calls moral ideals. Today people are enslaved by ideals of virtue. Ibsen shows that man is outgrowing his ideals, which must be challenged; conduct must justify itself by its effect upon happiness and not by its conformity to any rule or ideal. As man is always changing, there are no formulas for happiness and no valid, permanent systems of morals. By showing this in his plays, Ibsen is a great pioneer. Shaw claims that Ibsen's plays favour a natural morality similar to his own attitudes towards life. (Whether Ibsen indeed had such a philosophy is doubtful.) The vitality and energy of Ibsen's main characters are part of what Shaw terms the Life Force, an aspect of Creative Evolution.

Natural morality

Shaw believes that moral ideals are reflections of past social needs. Modern man has outgrown such needs and therefore the ideals of the past will cause unhappiness. Modern man has reached a stage where traditional notions of good and evil are no longer useful. What produces the most good and happiness should be regarded as moral. Such natural morality cannot be systematised into rules. Each person must decide for himself what is best according to the situation.

Creative Evolution

Because of his socialism and natural morality we might think that Shaw was simply a materialist or a political reformer. However, he had a strong, if unusual, religious streak in his character. He devised his own 'religion' based on Creative Evolution. According to Shaw, mankind is evolving towards a higher form of life which will result in an intellectual superman. While such evolution has always been the purpose of life, this new being will only come about because man's imagination wills it.

1892 to 1894

In 1892, the Independent Theatre was unable to find any new dramatists of the kind it sought and asked Shaw for a play. At the age of thirty-six he completed his first play, *Widowers' Houses*, one of three *Plays Unpleasant* treating social problems. In it he exposes the shady means by which the middle classes obtain their money through exploiting the poor living in the slums. The play is notable for its lack of a conventional happy ending and its lack of villains, as society is shown to be to blame. *Mrs Warren's Profession* (1893) had as its subject prostitution. It was banned from public performance by the censor. In the same year the Independent Labour Party was formed. Shaw wrote part of its programme. It was one of the groups that later formed the present English Labour Party.

In 1894 Shaw wrote *Arms and the Man* and *Candida*, his first important plays, at the request of friends who were formerly connected with the now defunct Independent Theatre. They were meant to be pleasant plays which, instead of treating social problems, would take the situations of conventional drama and contrast real life with the romantic attitudes common to the theatre of the time.

'Arms and the Man': first production

Arms and the Man was first produced on 21 April 1894 at the Avenue Theatre, London, and ran until 7 July 1894. The play was directed by Shaw. It was an immense hit with the audience and after the curtain fell there were enthusiastic cries for the author to come on stage. When Shaw appeared there was a single boo heard among the applause. Shaw said to the booer, 'I quite agree with you, my friend, but what are we two against so many?'.

The first production of *Arms and the Man* had only ten days of rehearsal. The actors were uncertain of their understanding of their parts and treated the play largely as a farce similar to the contemporary farces of W. S. Gilbert, which while mocking nineteenth-century platitudes were essentially cynically comic rather than humorously serious plays. No doubt the farcical treatment of *Arms and the Man* contributed to its success the first night. Shaw, however, felt the evening a disaster as the acting style destroyed the significance of his play. Solely to make

the audience laugh at false ideals and phoney sentiments would entertain but would not instruct. The play needed a more natural style of
acting if the audience were to see it was about real people and real life.
Its comedy results from the lifting of illusions, not from cynically
laughing at foolishness.

Although the play was considered a success, it was not immediately
popular and lost money on its first run. King Edward is said to have
disliked the play because it mocked army life. *Arms and the Man* was
taken on tour outside London in 1894 and in September there was an
American production. Although there were revivals, including and
the Granville Barker production of 1907, *Arms and the Man* was not
popular until after the First World War, when the returning soldiers
made people understand that war is not necessarily heroic. In 1932 the
play was filmed. A notable revival was in 1943; included in the cast were
such great actors as Laurence Olivier, Ralph Richardson and Sybil
Thorndike.

1895 to 1921

Arms and the Man and *Candida* were followed by a series of good plays
during the next six years. Shaw's best-known plays of this period
include *The Man of Destiny* (1895), *You Never Can Tell* (1896), *The
Devil's Disciple* (1897) and *Caesar and Cleopatra* (1898). Shaw also
wrote drama criticism, later reprinted as *Our Theatre in the Nineties,*
for *The Saturday Review* (1895–8).

Shaw married a rich socialist, Charlotte Payne-Townshend, in
1898.

His greatest work began in 1901 and included *Man and Superman*
(1901–2), *Major Barbara* (1905), *The Doctor's Dilemma* (1906),
Androcles and the Lion (1911–12), *Pygmalion* (1912), and *Heartbreak
House* (1916–17). His plays had 701 performances between 1904 and
1907 in productions by Granville Barker at the Court Theatre. This
established Shaw's reputation as a major dramatist.

The First World War appears to have affected him deeply and his
writing afterwards shows a decline. It is probable that the destruction
of the pre-war upper-middle class, which Shaw had known so well and
had tried to upset with his plays, destroyed part of his instinctive
relationship with the social world of his audience.

Among the plays of his major period, *Man and Superman* is best
known for the exposition of Shaw's philosophy of Creative Evolution.
Major Barbara shocked the socialists by making a rich capitalist

superior to various do-gooders. *Pygmalion*, another play which is still often performed, was recently used as the basis of the well-known musical comedy and film, *My Fair Lady*.

1921 to 1950

Back to Methuselah (1921) was Shaw's second attempt to expound his evolutionary philosophy through drama. *Saint Joan* (1923) was his most popular play. When asked whether he was becoming a Catholic, Shaw said, 'There's no room for two Popes in the Roman Catholic Church'. In 1925 he was awarded the Nobel Prize for Literature. *The Apple Cart* (1929) is felt by some to be Shaw's last important play, although he continued to write for the theatre until a few years before his death. In 1931 Shaw's collected works, the standard edition, began to be published. In the 1930s Shaw felt that the time was ripe to move from gradual political reform to a more radical, revolutionary socialism. He had always felt that socialism, rather than emerging from grass roots, would need strong leadership, and he was consequently attracted to the dictatorships of Mussolini in Italy and Stalin in Russia. He admired what he considered their efficiency and strength of will. Some of Shaw's more interesting late plays include *The Millionairess* (1936) and *In Good King Charles's Golden Days* (1939). A presentation of his political thought can be found in *Everybody's Political What's What?* (1944). When he was ninety, in 1946, Penguin Books published ten volumes of his work. One hundred thousand copies of each volume were printed. Shaw died on 2 November 1950 at the age of ninety-four.

The text of *Arms and the Man*

Arms and the Man was first published in 1898 as part of the second volume of *Plays Pleasant and Unpleasant*. Shaw added to his text full stage directions and character descriptions in italics so that the plays could be read as novels. To increase sales, each volume had a preface which only in part treated of the plays. Shaw's prefaces are used to express his opinions on many matters. A revised edition of the play was published in 1931. This is the standard edition as it incorporates changes Shaw made during productions of *Arms and the Man*.

Shaw's text has several unusual characteristics. He tries to avoid using italic type for spoken emphasis; in the place of italics he spaces out letters like this. Quotation marks as well as italic type are not used for titles of literary works or operas. Shaw also omits some apostrophes from contractions. Shaw's reason for such practices is that he wants his printed text to approximate to spoken speech. A few words are also spelled in slightly unconventional ways. In these *Notes* Shaw's spelling and punctuation are used in quotations from his work.

Another characteristic is the lack of a list of characters before the play. Shaw wants his readers to be introduced to characters as they appear in the play and not before. In *Arms and the Man* Captain Bluntschli's speeches are introduced by 'The Man' in Act I, as we have not been told his name. It is only in Act II when the Swiss soldier is identified that his speeches are introduced by 'Bluntschli'.

The title

The title, *Arms and the Man*, is taken from the opening line of Dryden's translation of Virgil's epic, the *Aeneid*. Dryden translates Virgil's 'Arma virumque cano' as 'Arms, and the man I sing'. Virgil's poem concerns heroism, public virtue, and the origins of the Roman Empire. Shaw's play, set in the early days of a new nation, Bulgaria, attempts to distinguish between true and false concepts of heroism, virtue, honour, and national dignity. It shows the difference between pretentious, romantic ideals and workable, human behaviour. It contrasts the reality of modern life with false literary portrayals of how people are supposed to conduct themselves.

The preface

The preface was written to attract readers for the publication in 1898 of *Candida*, *Arms and the Man*, *You Never Can Tell* and *The Man of Destiny* as *Plays Pleasant*. It contains some topics also discussed in the preface to *Plays Unpleasant*, also published in April 1898. The New Theatre movement had almost ended for a lack of new plays; consequently Shaw was asked to write dramas. Shaw claims theatre has become as important as schools or churches as a means of educating society. He then discusses his own plays. Romance and its ethical conventions must be destroyed in the theatre; romance breeds pessimism because people cannot live up to heroic ideals. Actors, who are often influenced by romantic parts, find his plays difficult to perform. Critics often dislike his plays, or claim not to understand them, because they want a romantic morality whereas his plays teach a natural morality. The behaviour of his Swiss officer in *Arms and the Man* can ᴏe proved as natural from military sources which show what warfare is really like. Liberal politicians object that he has insulted the new Balkan nations. Shaw claims the real issue is whether the Balkan states, newly emerging from Turkish domination, will survive the effect of Western European idealism. 'Idealism, which is only a flattering name for romance in politics and morals, is as obnoxious to me as romance in ethics or religion.' The tragedy and comedy of life result from founding institutions on ideals instead of the rational study of society and history.

The historical setting

The Bulgarian-Serbian War of 1882

The Ottoman, or Turkish, Empire controlled the Balkans from the fourteenth century until the mid-nineteenth century, when Serbia (now a part of Yugoslavia) became independent. In 1876 Bulgaria rebelled against the Turks and lost. The Russians declared war on the Turks in 1877 and in 1878 Bulgaria became an independent nation as a result of the Russo-Turkish War. In 1885 Eastern Rumelia, in the southern part of Bulgaria, revolted against Turkish rule and became united with Bulgaria. As a result Serbia invaded Bulgaria and in four days conquered a large part of the country. The Bulgarians, led by Prince Alᴄxander, fought back and with Russian aid made the Serbians retreat to Pirot, in Serbia, at which point the Austrians threatened to enter the war as Serbian allies.

Arms and the Man begins with the turning point of the war when the Serbians had advanced across the Dragoman Pass to Slivnitza in Bulgaria, where they lost a major battle on 17 November 1885. The second and third acts occur three days after the Treaty of Bucharest where, under Austrian pressure, a peace treaty was signed in which the Bulgarians had to return conquered Serbian territory. During the 1885 war the Serbs were led by Austrian officers, while the Bulgarians were led by Russians. Until the nineteenth century most wars were fought by mercenary professional soldiers and the practice still continued in the Balkans at this time. Switzerland had a long reputation for professional soldiers who would fight as mercenaries in any country, like Captain Bluntschli in *Arms and the Man*.

Part 2

Summaries
of ARMS AND THE MAN

A general summary

Act I

It is November 1885 in a small Bulgarian town during a war between Bulgaria and Serbia. Raina Petkoff, a young Bulgarian lady, is alone on her balcony. Her mother, Catherine, appears and says that Major Sergius Saranoff, to whom Raina is engaged, has led his cavalry in a major victory over the Serbs. Louka, a family servant, comes to warn Raina that the Serbian soldiers are fleeing towards the town and that as there may be shooting she must close her shutters.

Raina blows out her candle and retires to bed. A fugitive soldier from the Serbian Army opens her shutters, enters her room and lights a match. He tells Raina to keep quiet and light a candle or he will shoot. He warns her that he will be killed if he is caught. Hearing from voices outside that the Bulgarians are going to search the house, he puts down his pistol and admits he has lost. Raina then hides him from the soldiers who are searching the house. Louka sees the soldier's gun but says nothing.

The fugitive identifies himself as a professional soldier, Swiss by nationality. He is sceptical of heroism and tells Raina that Sergius's cavalry charge was suicidal. It was only because the Serbian machine-gunners were given the wrong ammunition that Sergius and his men were not slaughtered. The Swiss carries chocolates instead of bullets and being famished eats chocolates that Raina gives him. Raina calls him a 'chocolate cream soldier'. Raina and her mother help him to escape.

Act II

The second act takes place in March 1886, in the garden of the Petkoff house. Nicola, a middle-aged servant, tells Louka to be careful of her manners. If the Petkoffs realise that Louka does not respect them, Nicola cannot marry her. He must stay in their good graces if he is to start a shop in Sofia. The war is over and Major Petkoff and Sergius return. Sergius threatens to resign from the cavalry as his superior officers do not appreciate his heroic charge and will not promote him. Sergius and Major Petkoff exchange stories about a Swiss professional soldier who escaped after the famous cavalry charge with the aid of a young Bulgarian girl and her mother, who gave him a man's coat. Raina and her mother pretend to be shocked by the story.

Raina and Sergius speak to each other of their 'higher love', but shortly afterwards Sergius flirts with Louka, who mocks him by insinuating that Raina has had a lover while he was away. Angry, Sergius bruises Louka's arm.

The Swiss fugitive officer, Captain Bluntschli, surprises Catherine when he returns the coat. She tries hurriedly to get rid of him, but the Major and Sergius welcome him as an old acquaintance. Raina, surprised by his presence, exclaims, 'Oh! the chocolate cream soldier!', and then tries to hide her previous acquaintance with him. As Sergius and Major Petkoff need Bluntschli's practical professional advice on how to return soldiers to the provinces, they ask him to stay.

Act III

Act III takes place the same afternoon, after lunch, in the Petkoffs' library. Bluntschli writes plans for transporting the Bulgarian Army. Major Petkoff complains that his coat is lost; Nicola surprises the Major by producing the coat. Bluntschli and Raina, left alone, first discuss his escape and then her truthfulness. She says that she has only lied twice in her life. Bluntschli does not believe her. When helping him escape she put a portrait of herself, inscribed 'Raina, to her Chocolate Cream Soldier' in the pocket of her father's coat. Bluntschli did not see it and it may still be there. Bluntschli now receives telegrams saying that his father has died and he must return to Switzerland.

Nicola has planned to marry Louka but now realises that she may marry Sergius. Being practical he decides he will help her to marry Sergius if she will patronise the shop he plans to open. Sergius flirts with Louka who tells him that Raina loves Bluntschli. Sergius promises to marry Louka if he ever touches her again. Sergius challenges Bluntschli to a duel, which the latter mockingly evades. Raina guesses that Louka betrayed her to Sergius and she accuses the latter of using Louka as a spy. Angered, Raina says that Louka is probably listening at the door of the library. When Sergius opens the door Louka is there.

Raina removes her portrait from her father's coat, but he has already seen it. Bluntschli admits he is the chocolate cream soldier. The father is told by Raina that Sergius is in love with Louka; Nicola says that he is not engaged to Louka. Sergius apologises to Louka and, by kissing her hand, becomes, according to his promise, engaged to her. Bluntschli, who always thought Raina a romantic teenage girl, learns that she is a 23-year-old woman. He now wishes to marry her, but her parents object that he is neither noble nor rich. When Bluntschli impresses them with his inheritance they agree to the marriage. Raina momentarily objects, but then agrees to marry Bluntschli, who must leave for Switzerland on business. He promises to return in two weeks.

Detailed summaries

Act I

The stage directions of Act I, besides informing us that the scene is a lady's bedroom in a small Bulgarian town in 1885, offer insights into Raina and her society. The starlit, snowy mountains provide a romantic view, but are distant. The bedroom is a mixture of expensive traditional Bulgarian and cheap fashionable Viennese furnishing. Vienna, capital of the Austro-Hungarian Empire, was for the provincial Bulgarians a city of sophistication and high-class taste. The room has many good Eastern European decorations and fixtures: a painted wooden shrine with an ivory image of Christ, a Turkish settee, rich oriental tapestries and curtains. The furnishings imply that the inhabitants are badly imitating fashionable Western European culture, while the traditional Bulgarian, Eastern European and Turkish furnishings are, by contrast, natural to the region. Among the objects in the room are a box of chocolate creams and a portrait of a handsome officer. Both objects will be used prominently in Act I.

Raina, a young lady whose age we are not told until near the end of the play, stands on the balcony enjoying the beauty of the night. She is aware of her own beauty and, intensely conscious of the setting, attempts to lose herself in romantic feelings. Her mother, Catherine Petkoff, an energetic, attractive woman of forty, enters.

Shaw begins the play in the middle of the action, rather than with the events leading up to the action. The Bulgarians have won an important battle at Slivnitza over the Serbians. Sergius, Raina's intended husband, disobeyed the Russian officers who directed the Bulgarian Army and led his cavalry against the enemy, who scattered. Catherine calls Sergius a hero and criticises Raina for having delayed a year before becoming engaged to him. Raina previously doubted whether the ideals which she and Sergius had were anything more than dreams. While Sergius held her in his arms, she wondered whether their heroic talk was only the result of reading such romantic poets as Byron and Pushkin, and having been to the opera at Bucharest (capital of Rumania). Now his bravery shows that their ideals were right.

While Raina exclaims on her happiness, Louka enters. Louka is attractive and defiantly insolent, although a servant. The windows must be closed and the shutters locked because the Serbs may try to escape through the town. Raina wishes that people were not vengeful; she feels sorry for the fugitive Serbian soldiers. Left alone Raina holds up the portrait of Sergius and exclaims that she will never be unworthy of her hero. Shaw comments that Raina does not kiss the portrait or press it to her breast. She shows no sign of physical longing for Sergius.

Raina goes to bed and, when she hears gun-fire, blows out the candle. In the dark someone opens a broken shutter, enters the room and lights a match. A man (we are not told his name until Act II) warns Raina that if she raises an alarm she will be shot. He tells her to light a candle. She sees an 'undistinguished' soldier, a Serbian artillery officer. Raina, acting bravely, implies that she is not afraid to die. He says that may be so, but he doubts if she is willing, dressed in her nightgown, to call the drunken Bulgarian soldiers into her room to capture him. He has had a pistol in his hand, but now he throws it down on the ottoman (a cushioned seat like a sofa without a back) and takes from Raina the cloak which she was going to use to cover her nightgown. He clearly does not have Raina's idealism.

Soldiers beat on the front door of the house. Louka knocks on Raina's bedroom door and warns her to get up and open the door before the soldiers break it down. Inside the bedroom the man suddenly changes his attitude from being aggressive to sympathetic. He admits that he is trapped and now gives Raina her cloak to cover herself. Raina, acting on an impulsive mood of generosity, decides to help him to escape. She hides him behind a curtain and opens the door to Louka. Louka sees the man's pistol on the ottoman, but says nothing.

As the women are afraid of the drunken, wild Bulgarian soldiers entering the house, Catherine finds a Russian officer who will search Raina's room. Raina tells him that no one has tried to enter the room. She bravely opens the shutters to show there is no one on the balcony. Some shots are fired. The Russian believes her and leaves while Louka looks with curiosity at Raina.

After Catherine and Louka depart, the man announces that he is not a Serbian citizen. He is a professional soldier from Switzerland, hired by the Serbs. Raina sits on the pistol on the ottoman and shrieks with surprise at the narrow escape they had from being discovered. She mockingly offers the pistol back to the Swiss who grins and says it is not loaded. He has no ammunition; instead he carries chocolates in case he becomes hungry during a battle. Raina's ideals of courage, patriotism, and manhood are outraged. She insultingly offers him an opened box of candy which he, being starved, eats. He says that whereas young, inexperienced soldiers carry pistols and cartridges, old soldiers like himself carry food. When she contemptuously throws away the candy box, he jumps, afraid she will strike him. After three days under the fire of battle, he is extremely nervous.

Raina's idealistic attitude towards war is further challenged when the man says that only an amateur would have charged the Serbian machine-guns the way the Bulgarians did. If the Serbians could have fired, not a Bulgarian man or horse would have lived. Not knowing he has insulted Raina's fiancé, he mocks the leader of the Bulgarian cavalry charge, comparing him to an operatic tenor and to Don Quixote charging at windmills.

Raina, hurt but still believing in her fiancé's heroism, shows the Swiss her portrait of Sergius, the 'patriot and hero' she is going to marry. He begins to apologise but breaks out laughing at the ridiculous cavalry charge. He then suggests that Sergius might not have been foolish; perhaps he knew in advance about the Serbians having the wrong cartridges. This angers Raina further as it implies Sergius was a coward pretending to be brave.

Raina says that the Swiss is lucky she is not a professional soldier because he is at her mercy; she, however, will let him escape. When she tells him to climb down the waterpipe into the street, he almost faints from fear of being chased again. He tells her to call the soldiers instead. Raina says he is 'a very poor soldier: a chocolate cream soldier!' and pities him. Not having rested in two days he begins to fall asleep.

Raina says she will help him. She starts to brag about her honour and explains that they are a rich, well-known family. He pretends to be impressed. Each of her boasts unintentionally shows how provincial and rural Bulgaria is. Theirs is the only house with a flight of stairs, two rows of windows, and a library. The family goes to Bucharest each year for the opera. She mentions Verdi's *Ernani*. (*Ernani*, 1844, is an operatic version of Victor Hugo's romantic play, *Hernani*.) Raina says that she and her mother have the same sense of honour as the old Castilian noble in the opera who saves his bitterest enemy. Pretending a similar nobility of conduct, she claims that she would have earlier saved the soldier if he had said that he was a fugitive. He doubts this. Whereas Raina is inspired by high romantic ideals of noble behaviour, the Swiss is unromantic and full of common sense. Being practical he suggests that he could not afford to depend on such noble gestures. We now learn that his father owns six hotels, which is unusual for a professional soldier working in a foreign army. There is something out of the ordinary, still unexplained, about him.

When Raina starts to go in search of her mother the soldier begins to fall asleep. Seeing this she is insulted and asks him to stand all the time while she is out of the room. He agrees but falls asleep on her bed as soon as she leaves. Once more Shaw contrasts her romantic idealism with the realities of life. Raina returns with her mother who is shocked at seeing the soldier asleep on her daughter's bed. When the mother tries to wake him, Raina surprises her by saying that 'the poor darling' is tired and should be let sleep.

COMMENTARY: The opening scene is similar to a prologue in making us aware of several important facts that form the basis of Shaw's theme. Raina and Sergius have been influenced by English and Russian romantic writers and the opera into holding idealistic, even visionary, views about life. Raina, however, is not a completely unpractical romantic since she has had doubts about the possibility of attaining such ideals. Shaw's aim in the play is to deflate unrealistically romantic notions of heroism and bravery.

Act I is a comedy of reversals in which Raina's romantic idealism is continually challenged by the professional soldier's common sense and experience of life. At first he seems brutal; he threatens Raina with a pistol. He uses the fact that she is in nightclothes to prevent her from calling for the Bulgarian soldiers, and he keeps her from covering herself with a cloak. But when he thinks the Bulgarian soldiers are in any case going to search the room he starts to act like a gentleman. His threats were fake; he did not even have bullets in his gun. Being more concerned with survival than heroism, he carries chocolate instead of bullets.

Romantic heroism is also mocked by his description of the cavalry charge Sergius led. To Raina the charge was an act of bravery; to the professional soldier it was an act of stupidity deserving punishment. Although Raina speaks of honour she lies to the Russian officer that no one has tried to enter her room. The deception of the Russian officer shows idealism failing again when he believes her word and fails to search the room.

Raina's idealised view of herself is shown by her description of her family's sophistication. The soldier is clearly not impressed by the Petkoff library, staircase, and windows. His father, who owns six hotels, would know many more comforts. Raina's attempt to make the soldier act bravely is also shown to be foolish as she really does not want him to risk death by escaping at night. Pretending to save him out of nobility of conduct, she in fact pities him and is, as we learn later, romantically attracted to him despite his absolute lack of the idealism she associates with her fiancé, Sergius. Throughout the act we have seen her both infatuated with romantic, heroic idealism and full of common sense when dealing with practical matters, such as saving the soldier.

The professional soldier distrusts all ideals and acts realistically about life. Nervous and exhausted after a three-day siege, he cannot keep up a brave front. The soldier's attachment to chocolates, which were in the late-nineteenth century considered a luxury for women, is meant to be shocking and gives point to Raina's feeling that he is a comic parody of the brave soldier of her ideals. If he carried bread, dried meat, or another sensible ration, he would be less pitiful, and the play would be less funny.

If Raina and the Swiss soldier seem to represent the opposite extremes of romantic idealism and practical realism, there are hints that the situation may not be as obvious as it first appears. Why did Raina originally have doubts about Sergius's heroism and why is she so helpful towards the Swiss soldier? Does she really save him because of noble ideals or is she in some way attracted to him? And why should he, the son of a well-to-do hotel owner, be serving as a professional soldier in the Serbian Army?

Shaw uses coincidence more often than most writers as a way of advancing his plot. The coincidence of the escaped soldier taking refuge from the Bulgarians in the bedroom of the fiancé of the cavalry officer who defeated the Serbians, takes us directly into a conflict of personalities and sets up the subsequent events in the play.

The act is an example of anti-climax, a favourite Shavian comic device (in which a lame or trivial ending is supplied to a course of events—or a sentence or passage—which promised to reach a climax). The opening announcement of dangerous escaped fugitives ends in a pitiful escapee sleeping on Raina's bed. A close study of most events or scenes within the act will show that they end with anti-climaxes.

Act II

It is 6 March 1886, a little over three months after the events of Act I, in the garden of the Petkoff house. There is laundry hanging out on the fruit bushes, suggesting the lack of refined manners among the Petkoffs. The lasting Turkish influence on the region is shown by the sight of the top of some minarets in the distance and a Turkish coffee pot on a table laid for breakfast. Louka, the servant, is smoking a cigarette, an example of her defiance, and listening with displeasure to Nicola, a middle-aged male servant. Nicola is cold, calculating, and cunning. As the act begins he warns Louka against defying the Petkoffs. If she is dismissed Nicola will not marry her; he must depend on the influential family to be good customers at the shop he hopes to open in Sofia, the capital of Bulgaria. Louka complains that he has no spirit. She intimates that as she knows family secrets no one would dare to dismiss her. Nicola asks who would believe her; he also knows secrets that would cause Sergius to break his engagement to Raina. Louka is surprised into revealing her secret. In contrast to Louka's defiant attitude, Nicola claims that keeping secrets is the best way for a servant to get ahead. Louka replies that he has the soul of a servant. This scene gives us excellent portraits of the two characters.

A male voice is heard. It is Major Petkoff unexpectedly returned from the wars. Major Petkoff is a cheerful, unsophisticated man of about fifty. Shaw's stage directions say that he likes money, his family, and his place in local society, but is otherwise unambitious. Although proud to have been a major in the Bulgarian Army, he is glad to return home. Petkoff tells Nicola to inform the family that he is home. (Notice how Shaw gets characters offstage when they are not needed. Nicola tells Louka to fetch some fresh coffee; Major Petkoff sends Nicola off to get some fresh coffee. Because fetching fresh coffee is used as an excuse for their exits, Shaw turns 'fresh coffee' into a continuing joke.)

Catherine enters. She is casually dressed but attractive. She welcomes her husband with a kiss and asks if he has had some fresh coffee. Petkoff informs her that the powerful Austrians have forced the Bulgarians to sign a peace treaty with the Serbians. Catherine, a fanatical patriot, argues that her husband should have annexed Serbia and made Prince Alexander (the ruler of Bulgaria) Emperor of the Balkan countries. He jokingly replies that to do so he would have first needed to conquer the Austrian Empire (which opposed Bulgarian expansion) and this would have kept him away from home for too long.

Catherine and the Major exchange domestic talk. Catherine says that the Major is a barbarian; she hopes that he behaved well in front of the Russian officers. The Major answers that he told them he had a library. When Catherine says she had an electric bell installed to call the servants from the kitchen, he asks why not shout for them. They discuss the ways of civilisation, each laughing at the other for still having peasant habits; she hangs washing to dry where visitors can see it. Although Catherine is usually the dominant figure and has social pretensions, the Major holds his own ground through being good-natured and amused.

Major Sergius Saranoff is announced. Major Petkoff does not like Sergius and thinks him an incompetent soldier. He complains that Sergius wants Petkoff to make him a general. When Catherine says that the country should have one Bulgarian general, Petkoff replies that Sergius cannot be promoted so long as there is a chance of war occurring again.

Sergius is tall, romantic, and handsome. He is strong, high-spirited, and imaginative. Shaw describes him as a clever, untamed barbarian who has been strongly affected by the influence of Western civilisation in the Balkans; the 'result' is similar to what early nineteenth-century thought produced in England, Byronism. Brooding on the failure of himself and others to live up to ideals results in cynicism and scorn. Disappointed, Sergius has a partly tragic, partly ironic attitude towards life. He is mocking, moody and has an 'air of mystery' such as that with which Byron's poetic hero, Childe Harold, fascinated early nineteenth-century readers. He is idealised as a hero by both Raina and her mother.

According to Catherine, everyone is wild over Sergius's heroism in leading the cavalry charge. He says, ironically, that it was the beginning and end of his reputation as a soldier; the Russian officers disapprove of unprofessional bravery—while he was winning the battle the wrong way the Russian generals were losing it the right way. Two Russian colonels who lost their regiments by following the principles of scientific warfare have been promoted to major-generals, whereas he is still a major. He has, therefore, sent in his resignation from the army. (Shaw's own irony is complex here. He is mocking the professional soldiers for their so-called 'science' of warfare and their resentment at someone winning a battle by untrained means. But Shaw is also mocking Sergius's Byronic attitudinising in making himself appear superior to the professionals whom he cynically treats as stupid.) When Catherine tells him to withdraw his resignation, Sergius says 'I never withdraw'. We never hear anything more about Sergius's resignation after this scene.

Raina enters, partly dressed in Turkish style with a gold cap. She acts in a queenly manner and Sergius kneels down to kiss her hand. Her mother, who is not deceived by Raina's posturing, remarks that her dramatic entrances are planned. Raina listens for the 'right moment' to make a grand entrance. Sergius leads Raina 'with splendid gallantry' to the table, where she welcomes her father.

Sergius mocks professional soldiers who attack when stronger than the enemy and avoid conflict when weaker. Major Petkoff replies that soldiering is just a trade like any other business. Sergius has no desire to be a tradesman; on the advice of a Swiss captain he has decided to give up soldiering. The Swiss captain is, of course, Raina's chocolate cream soldier. Raina and Catherine ask questions about this Swiss soldier. The Swiss tricked Major Petkoff into exchanging fifty Serbian soldiers for two hundred aged horses that were so useless they could not even be eaten. Raina asks what the Swiss was like and is told by Sergius that he was just a travelling salesman in a uniform. Sergius tells the women a story he heard about how the Swiss escaped after the Serbian defeat at Slivnitza.

Sergius ironically calls the story a 'romance'. The Swiss escaped Sergius's cavalry by climbing a waterpipe into the bedroom of a young woman. The Bulgarian lady 'entertained him' for an hour and afterwards called in her mother to dispel any wrong impressions about what she had been doing. (Sergius, of course, does not know Raina is the young lady and mistakenly assumes that the hour was not spent innocently.) The young lady and her mother helped the Swiss to escape by disguising him in a coat belonging to the husband who was away in the Bulgarian Army.

Raina and Catherine object that the story is too coarse to tell in front of women. Sergius immediately apologises; life, he says, has made him cynical. Major Petkoff says that a soldier's daughter should be able to put up with a little reality. In any case the problem now is to get three regiments back to Philippopolis, capital of the Rumelian province, as there is no fodder for them along the Sofia route. The Major goes offstage from the garden towards the house with Catherine who has skilfully manoeuvered Sergius into staying behind with Raina.

Raina, alone with Sergius, begins acting like a character in a romantic opera. She calls him her hero and king; she says he is worthy of any woman and was never absent from her thoughts for a moment. He calls her his queen and saint, kisses her forehead, and says she inspired him 'like a knight in a tournament' who fights with his lady looking on. Louka enters the garden from the house to clear the breakfast table. Raina exits to find her hat in order that she and Sergius can go for a walk. Sergius says that if Raina is away for five minutes it will seem like five hours.

But as soon as Raina is offstage Sergius starts trying to attract the attention of Louka. He twirls his moustache, swaggers, and then says to her that 'higher love' is fatiguing and one needs relief. Pretending not to understand, she offers him coffee. Sergius grabs her hand and slips his arm around her waist. When he will not let her go, Louka sensibly tells him to stand where they cannot be seen.

Louka suggests that Raina might be spying on them from a window. When Sergius tries to kiss her she says that the aristocrats are all alike; both Sergius and Raina cheat each other. Sergius falls for the bait and becomes upset. He tells Louka not to speak of Raina; but he soon asks who his rival is. Louka says she does not know the name but heard his voice in Raina's room; if the man comes to the house again Raina will marry him whether he 'likes it or not'. The difference, Louka says, is obvious between real passion and the false love Raina and Sergius pretend.

Sergius grabs Louka's arms, hurting her, and accuses her of dishonouring him. He calls her dirt with the soul of a servant, a remark which hurts her further as she herself had used the same expression earlier against Nicola. Angered, she calls Raina a liar and claims to be worth six of Raina. Sergius tries to apologise for hurting her, but Louka says that apologies may satisfy a lady but are of no use to a servant. Feeling mocked, he tries to pay her with money, but she refuses and grandly offers him her arm to kiss. Realising that she is acting as an equal, he says 'Never!'. She picks up the tray with dignity and goes to the house. It seems that Sergius is less heroic and noble-minded than he pretends, while Louka, despite differences in social position, is his equal in strength of will and pride.

Raina returns and seeing Sergius upset says laughingly that he must have been flirting with Louka. Sergius denies it and kisses her hand. Catherine enters and asks Sergius to go to the library to help her husband make plans for sending the three regiments to Philippopolis.

As soon as Catherine and Raina are alone the mother remarks on the difficulty that Raina caused by helping the Swiss to escape. Major Petkoff has asked for the old coat they gave to the Swiss soldier. Raina says that the Swiss is a beast to have told others about his escape. If he ever came to the house again, she would stuff him so full of chocolate creams that he would strangle. Catherine, unimpressed, asks how long the soldier was in Raina's room before she called her mother. Raina pretends to forget how long and starts to give confused replies. Catherine says that Sergius will break the engagement if he finds out about the escapade. Raina sarcastically replies that since Sergius is Catherine's pet, she wishes Catherine could marry him. She would like to shock Sergius out of his stuffy dignity. (This parallels Sergius's remark about higher love being fatiguing.) She wishes he would find out. Raina walks away leaving Catherine shocked.

Louka returns and takes a calling card out of her blouse and puts it on a tray where it should have been. A gentleman has called and asked to see the lady of the house. Catherine looks at the man's calling card and reads 'Captain Bluntschli'. Louka says it is a Swiss name. Catherine immediately realises it is the Swiss soldier returning the coat. What a time for him to return! Hoping to get rid of the man quickly before her husband and Sergius know he is there, she asks Louka to bring him to the garden. Louka goes to the house and returns with Captain Blunt-schli. As soon as Louka starts to leave, Catherine asks him to depart because, she pretends, her husband and future son-in-law would be angry to find an enemy soldier in the house. She says that if her husband 'discovers our secret' he will never forgive her and may kill his daughter, an unlikely turn of events from what we know of the Major. Catherine, like her daughter, has no hesitation about lying when in uncomfortable situations. Bluntschli turns to leave by way of the house, but Catherine grabs him and directs him out by way of the stable gates.

Suddenly Major Petkoff rushes from the house and, bringing to an anti-climax Catherine's fears of what will happen when the Swiss is discovered, greets him as 'My dear Captain Bluntschli'. Even Sergius welcomes 'our friend the enemy'. While Catherine makes excuses for the Swiss to depart quickly, the men ask Bluntschli to stay and give his professional advice on how to send their three regiments to Philippop-olis. Bluntschli immediately understands the transport problem and goes off with Sergius and Major Petkoff towards the house to work.

Raina comes from the house, sees Bluntschli and exclaims in delight. 'Oh! The chocolate cream soldier!' Everyone is startled. Raina tries to cover up her remark about the chocolate cream soldier; she claims that she was thinking about a chocolate ornament for a sweet dessert that she made that morning which Nicola ruined by accident. Major Petkoff is suspicious of all the odd events. First Nicola appears to have taken Captain Bluntschli to the garden instead of the library to meet him. Then Raina says she was cooking that morning, although she never cooked before. And Nicola, who is always careful, has broken Raina's chocolate soldier!

At just this moment Nicola enters and places a bag before Bluntschli. It is the bag in which Bluntschli brought the coat he is returning. A comic scene develops as Nicola rightly says that he is only obeying Catherine's orders to return the bag to Bluntschli while Catherine, fear-ing the deception will be discovered, says she never told him to bring Bluntschli's luggage to the garden. Swiftly understanding Catherine's attempt to deceive the others, Nicola humbly excuses himself while Major Petkoff calls him a donkey. Major Petkoff calms down and asks Bluntschli to stay at the house for a while. When Bluntschli accepts the invitation everyone smiles except Catherine, who makes a face of despair.

COMMENTARY: Act II is also a comedy of reversals involving intrigue, illusions, and reality. Sergius pretends to love Raina, but is soon flirting with Louka. Major Petkoff and Sergius have learned that their Swiss friend, Captain Bluntschli, was helped to escape from the Bulgarians by two women, but they do not know the women were Raina and Catherine. Both women pretend to be shocked by the story of the Swiss soldier's escape but are worried that Major Petkoff will realise that the reason his coat is missing is that it was given to the Swiss. Soon Bluntschli appears at the house trying to return the coat. While Catherine attempts to get him quickly away, the Major and Sergius find him and welcome him as a friend. Meanwhile, Catherine, who is afraid that Sergius may break his engagement to Raina, is shocked to realise that Raina does not care about the engagement. Louka, the servant girl, is clearly out to win Sergius. Nicola, who is engaged to marry Louka, is mostly concerned with opening a shop. In various situations Nicola pretends to act foolishly so as to take suspicion away from Raina and Catherine.

We are struck by the coincidence of the two men having met the Swiss soldier and by the comic situation of their knowing the circumstances of his escape without realising that their wife and fiancée were involved. Shaw is a master of using coincidences in a play both for comic effects and to set up situations from which the subsequent action follows.

Shaw's description of Sergius should be studied closely. With his good looks, excessive gallantry and noble affectations, Sergius is a complete contrast, both in appearance and personality, to the practical, unheroic Swiss soldier whom Raina helped in Act I. In satirising the romantic idealism of Sergius and Raina, Shaw is, of course satirising the continuing influence of romantic idealism on late nineteenth-century England. Sergius's cynical attitude towards life results from having ideals which are impractical and unrealistic. Shaw's point of view is that idealism is not only false because it is unworkable, but it also creates despair and cynicism. If the professional soldier in Act I is contrasted with Raina's heroic ideals of war, in Act II we are aware of a contrast between Raina's idealistic posturing and Louka's contempt for Sergius's supposed superiority. Both Raina and Sergius are, in fact, bored with their game of idealistic love but feel they must pretend in public. Louka is determined to marry above her social class and to convince Sergius that she is his equal.

Act III

Act III is set in the library the same day after lunch. The library, of which the Petkoffs are proud, is another anti-climax. There is a single shelf of old novels and two small decorative shelves with books that have obviously been given as gifts. The wall is mostly covered by trophies from war and hunting. In spite of all the Petkoffs' bragging about their library, it is obviously used mostly as a sitting room, although the few books are well-thumbed and must have been read and re-read. They know a little literature very well, and this has been a source of their ideas. Sergius is sitting at the table, nibbling the feather of a quill pen while watching Bluntschli working over some maps and writing instructions. He envies Bluntschli's common-sense, businesslike way of working, but is irritated because he feels he should not esteem the prosaic.

Major Petkoff is happy to be home from the wars; he only needs his old coat to make him feel comfortable. Catherine claims that the old coat must be hanging in the blue closet. He says he has looked for it and tells Catherine that he will wager any piece of jewellery she wants against her housekeeping money for a week that the coat is not in the closet. Catherine accepts. Petkoff, excited by the idea of gambling, tries to take other bets on the coat. He is willing to bet Sergius an Arabian mare, but Catherine, now concerned at his losing money to others, warns her husband that an Arabian mare will cost 50,000 levas. As they argue, Nicola returns with the coat from the closet.

Bluntschli finishes his work and hands the last orders to Petkoff, who is surprised at and envious of his speed. Bluntschli, obviously in command, gives Sergius instructions. The latter obeys begrudgingly; he prefers wild, unthinking bravery to such unheroic, professional soldiery. Bluntschli sends Petkoff to make certain Sergius gives his orders and Petkoff asks Catherine to come along as she will instil more discipline in the soldiers!

Raina looks mischievously at Bluntschli and asks if his soldiers were angry at his 'running away from Sergius's charge'; Bluntschli grins and says that the troops were happy he fled as they themselves had run away. Raina says that her father and Sergius heard a story about him escaping with the aid of two Bulgarian women. Luckily they do not know Bluntschli hid in Petkoff's house; if they did Sergius would certainly kill Bluntschli in a duel. Bluntschli does not take her remarks seriously and advises her not to tell them. Raina puts on her noble manner and claims that she does not wish to deceive Sergius. She wants a beautiful, perfect relationship with him in which there will be no deceit. Bluntschli reminds her of the deceitful story she told about the sweet pudding that morning.

Raina claims she had only lied twice in her life and both times were to save Bluntschli's life. Bluntschli belittles this. Raina becomes indignant and accuses him of ingratitude and unfaithfulness; she says he is incapable of any noble sentiments. She paces around the room, acts tragically, and claims that he will never understand how women hate to lie. Bluntschli calmly replies that, as much as he admires her, he does not believe a word she says. Apparently shocked, she asks if he realises what he has said. He says he does. Pointing to herself she starts to exclaim indignantly, then realising that he is not impressed she sits suddenly beside him and asks in a friendly, confiding manner, 'How did you find me out?'.

Raina's admission is the turning point in the play. Somewhat confused, she says that Bluntschli is the first man who has not taken her seriously. He says that on the contrary he speaks seriously to her whereas others just played her games. Raina admits that she has always adopted a 'noble attitude' and used a 'thrilling voice'. Her nurse, her parents, and Sergius believed she was sincere. Bluntschli remarks that Sergius acts that way himself. Raina is shocked to realise that Sergius may also be play-acting.

Raina asks Bluntschli what he thought when he found her portrait in the pocket of the coat. He is stunned. He never found the portrait; it must still be in Major Petkoff's coat. Raina is badly upset as she wrote a message to her chocolate cream soldier on the portrait. Trying to decide whether the portrait is still in the coat, she asks him whether anyone else touched it. He shocks her by saying that at one time he pawned the coat as a means of keeping it safe.

Louka brings Bluntschli four telegrams. He learns that his father has died, leaving him a fortune. He must return to Switzerland immediately to look after his business interests. Louka remarks that Bluntschli does not show any grief. Raina asks what is to be expected from a soldier and leaves the room.

Louka's left sleeve is held up on her shoulder with a brooch. Her arm is naked except for a bracelet covering the bruise Sergius made. Nicola enters and comments on the 'fashion' of the way she is wearing her sleeve. He shows her some money. Sergius gave him twenty levas for no reason. He calls Sergius a fool. Bluntschli gave him ten levas for covering up the lies of Catherine and Raina. Nicola says Bluntschli is no fool. Louka accuses Nicola of selling his manhood for thirty levas. She claims that she was not born to be a servant; when he has his shop he will be everybody's servant. He says that when they are married he will be master in his own house. She replies that he will never be master of her house.

Nicola suddenly becomes serious and lectures Louka. She has great ambitions, but if she catches a rich husband she must remember Nicola

taught her how to behave like a lady instead of a peasant. He thinks
Sergius might marry her and then Louka could become one of the best
customers in his shop, instead of being a wife and costing Nicola money.
Louka says he would rather serve her than be her husband; he has the
soul of a servant. He ignores the insult and continues to lecture her. If
she wants to become a lady by marrying richly she should stop acting so
insultingly towards him. Insults show a kind of affection and will ruin
her chances of winning a rich husband. Besides, only peasants act high
and mighty towards servants. A lady acts as if she expected to have her
own way and does not fight. A lady is like a servant, she knows her place.
In reply Louka orders him to put the logs on the fire. Sergius enters and
Nicola leaves, telling Louka to clean the table.

Sergius immediately goes to Louka and examines the bruise he made
earlier on her arm. He attempts to embrace her, but she reprimands him.
An officer should behave better. She asks him if he is sorry and he folds
his arms, as he will do many times in Act III, and says 'I am never sorry'.
She asks if the poor are less brave than the rich. He says that people are
like dogs; they are both brave and afraid of their masters. Louka says he
does not know what real courage is. Real courage is to marry someone
you love regardless of what others think. If she were the Empress of
Russia she would marry Sergius if she loved him, even though he would
be socially beneath her. She says he would not do the same; he would
marry a rich man's daughter instead. Louka has challenged Sergius's
notion of his courage and nobility by saying he is not brave enough to
marry beneath his social station. He immediately reacts; he would
marry her if he loved her, but he loves Raina instead. Louka says Raina
will never marry him now that the Swiss soldier has returned; the Swiss
is worth ten of Sergius. Sergius is not good enough for Louka; she
would not marry Sergius if he did ask.

Sergius grabs her, saying he will kill the Swiss. Perhaps, she taunts
him, he will kill you. He has beaten Sergius in love, maybe he will also
win in fighting. Sergius is tormented by the thought of Raina deceiving
him. Louka reminds him that he is deceiving Raina by having his arms
around her. Sergius as usual is confused by the discrepancy between his
ideals and his actions. He dramatises his despair at not being able to
live a life of ideals; he threatens to commit suicide. He tells Louka that
if he ever touches her again he will marry her.

Bluntschli enters with some papers in his hand. Sergius immediately
challenges him to a duel. Bluntschli is unimpressed and says that as the
choice of weapons is his, he will use a machine-gun. Sergius is affronted.
Bluntschli eventually agrees to fight by sword; however, he will not use
a horse as horses are too dangerous. Raina rushes in asking why they

are going to fight. Bluntschli does not know why; it was Sergius's idea. Sergius accuses Bluntschli of making love to Raina. Bluntschli tells him to apologise. Again folding his arms, Sergius once more says, 'I never apologize', and claims that war and love are frauds. Raina wonders who told Sergius about that night in November. Suddenly she realises it was Louka. Angry, she says that she had looked out the window (remember Louka accused her of spying!) and saw Sergius making love to Louka. Sergius says life is a farce and announces that he will not fight Bluntschli, who has no sense of honour. Bluntschli calmly ignores the vulgar quarrel that develops between Raina and Sergius. Raina and Sergius quieten down somewhat, annoyed by Bluntschli's calmness .When Raina claims that Louka is probably eavesdropping at the door, Sergius opens the door where Louka is indeed found snooping. Louka says she is not ashamed to be caught spying as she loves . . . Major Petkoff enters before she can finish saying whom.

Raina, pretending to be an affectionate daughter, takes the coat from her father, finds the photograph in the pocket and tosses it to Bluntschli, who hides it. Petkoff looks into the pocket, cannot find the photograph, and wonders what happened to it. He has read the inscription from Raina 'to her Chocolate Cream Soldier' and has guessed it refers to Bluntschli, who confesses what happened. Raina, still annoyed, announces that Sergius is going to marry Louka.

Louka suddenly takes command of the situation by playing upon Sergius's absurd sense of dignity and manoeuvring him into a position where, according to his ideals, he must marry her. She claims to be insulted and demands an apology from Sergius, who immediately folds his arms and prepares to say 'no'. When Bluntschli reminds her that Sergius never apologises, she replies that while he will not apologise to his equal, he cannot refuse to apologise to a poor servant. This strikes exactly the right note; Sergius, acting gallantly, kneels down and asks her forgiveness. Louka cautiously extends her hand. As soon as he kisses her hand she reminds him of his earlier pledge to marry her if he touched her again. To complete her victory she offers to allow him to withdraw his pledge if he wishes. He, honourably, says 'Withdraw! Never!', and engages to marry her.

Louka now claims that Raina loves Bluntschli. Bluntschli denies it, saying that he is just a soldier, a vagabond, who has ruined his life through 'an incurably romantic disposition'. Sergius is stunned by the notion of the prosaic Bluntschli thinking of himself as a romantic. Bluntschli says he ran away from home, went into the army instead of his father's business and even came back to look at Raina again. He asks how anyone could think that a pretty 17-year-old girl like Raina would fall in love with a 34-year-old soldier like himself. He holds up the portrait and asks whether any woman seriously involved in an affair would write 'Raina, to her Chocolate Cream Soldier: A Souvenir'. Raina calls him a romantic idiot! Does he not realise that she is a woman of twenty-three and not a schoolgirl of seventeen?

Stunned, but rapidly understanding the situation and the reasons behind past events, Bluntschli tries to propose to Raina. Catherine objects as the Petkoffs are one of the most important families in Bulgaria. Asserting an aristocratic pedigree, she says their position can be traced back twenty years. Major Petkoff also objects that Raina is used to living richly. Bluntschli tells them of all the hotel equipment he has inherited. The catalogue of riches is very funny and includes 2,400 eider-down quilts. It is much more than anyone in Bulgaria owns. Petkoff, stunned, asks if he is Emperor of Switzerland. Bluntschli replies that in Switzerland the highest rank is to be a free citizen. Raina sulks at this show of being sold. Bluntschli faces her and asks her whom she loves; she is reminded that he is her 'chocolate cream soldier'. He takes this as her acceptance of marrying him and, after looking at his watch, becomes suddenly businesslike. He gives Petkoff some further instructions about troop transport and leaves saying he will return in two weeks.

COMMENTARY: The third act shows the characters in new perspectives. Nicola, who seemed a down-trodden servant, acts magnificently in advancing Louka's prospects of marrying Sergius. Major Petkoff also surprises us by having understood, without having previously revealed it, that Raina helped Bluntschli to escape. Raina surprises us by her admission to Bluntschli that she has been posing all her life.

Bluntschli also changes in Act III. We see him as a highly efficient, professional soldier, who understands how to command people and give explicit orders. He gains our respect. He is not frightened by Sergius's threat to kill him. Being a professional, he hates to fight unnecessarily, but if he must fight he will, and being well trained and unemotional he expects to win. Instead of the cowardly, pitiful, hunted man of Act I, we see someone with authority and manliness greater than the false heroism of Sergius. But having decided Bluntschli is perhaps too overwhelmingly a realist and too secure in life to have our sympathies, we are shocked to realise that he is also, by his own admission, a romantic. He ran away from home, gave up his father's good business to join the army, romantically climbed into Raina's room instead of hiding in some less dangerous place, and has now returned to see her. Moreover, he has no idea that Raina acted to save him because she is attracted to him. Raina, by hiding him, could have lost her reputation in her society and never married. It would have been felt that she slept with an enemy soldier, while engaged to marry Sergius. Bluntschli mistakes her behaviour for a schoolgirl's romantic dream of adventure. This rightly angers Raina. She saved Bluntschli because she fell in love with him; she pitied him, was attracted to his weaknesses, his common sense, his disagreeable truthfulness, as well as to the romantic escapade of his climbing into her room in hope of protection.

Bluntschli has risen in our evaluation in Act III until the end, when we suddenly see that he is perhaps the only one who has not understood the nature of Raina's behaviour towards himself. However, he immediately regains our high opinion by overcoming Raina's scruples against marrying him, and by again revealing his ability to take command. Instead of acting romantically about Raina, he leaves immediately to clear up his business in Switzerland, after giving further instructions about the Bulgarian troops, and says he will return in two weeks, presumably to marry Raina. The same common sense and rationality which made him appear mean and pitiful in Act I, when he was escaping, now make him appear larger than life. Instead of the brave cavalry commander as hero, we have the brisk, efficient businessman as hero.

Sergius never changes during the play and will marry Louka as a result of the same high ideals of noble conduct that brought about his suicidal cavalry charge in Act I.

We must distinguish between romanticism as a code of behaviour involving high-flying ideals, and being romantic in the sense of acting with warmth or affection towards others. Shaw was against false ideals and pretended sentiments; he was not against love and affection. If Raina was romantic in dreaming of Sergius's heroism, she was generous and romantic in saving Bluntschli's life in November. Such romanticism—the ability to love, to feel warmth towards others—is what makes her personality attractive. She has energy and vitality that will not stay limited by social or moral conventions. While common-sense realism has triumphed over romantic ideals, realism is shown to be false if it does not take into account such human affections as love.

Part 3

Commentary

The theatre of the 1890s

The theatre of the time was dominated by romantic historical drama and well-made but insignificant comedies. The romantic dramas indoctrinated high, noble ideals of conduct. The comedies cynically laughed at people unable to live up to such ideals. Two fashionable kinds of comedy were 'the well-made play', influenced by the French writer, Victorien Sardou, and the satiric comedies of W.S. Gilbert. The well-made play consisted of complicated plots in which one incident led quickly to another. Such plays often dealt in deceptions which became more and more complicated until some unexpected event happily resolved the situation with a laugh. Gilbert's plays, of which *Engaged* is the best known, cynically mocked the high ideals of romantic drama and Victorian society. They used the high-flying situations and exaggerated language of romantic drama, which they parodied. Set against such idealism, the characters were shown at key moments to calculate crudely the financial advantages of love, marriage and friendship. The attitude of such plays was, frankly, cynical.

Shaw's relationship to such kinds of theatre can be seen in *Arms and the Man*, where he uses the romantic setting of a war in Bulgaria. Although his aim and intention are different, he uses the Gilbertian technique of parodying the romantic. (His victorious hero is a bad soldier; Bulgaria is a rough peasant society.) As in Gilbert, the discrepancy between idealised sentiments and behaviour is humorous. Shaw shows people, despite their noble language, acting in self-interest. He, however, sees such conduct as natural and praiseworthy rather than mocking it. Shaw makes fun of false ideals and not of the insincerities of his characters.

The critical reception and Shaw's intentions

It is common to the history of the arts that when a new style or attitude appears it is interpreted and judged by the standards of art that were last popular. William Archer, a friend of Shaw's, reviewed *Arms and the Man* in *The World* (25 April 1894) and saw the play as similar to Gilbert's satiric comedies. Archer claimed that Shaw was preoccupied by 'the seamy side of the human mind'. He felt that such cynicism limited art. Archer praised Act I of *Arms and the Man* as knocking 'the stuffing so to speak, out of war' by contrasting a romantic girl's ideal of battle with 'the sordid reality as it appears to a professional soldier'. He objects that in Act II Raina is a different character; she is a 'deliberate humbug' without any genuine emotions. Archer claims that it is unnatural for Sergius to analyse his various moods before Louka, and that Shaw has dehumanised his characters by showing only their pettiness. Archer says that while he agrees with Shaw that people have deluded themselves with idealised notions of romantic love, it is wrong to show Raina transferring her affections so rapidly in a few hours 'from a man whom she thought she had adored for years to one whom she has only once before set eyes on'.

Shaw answered Archer in two letters. He denied that his plays were cynical farces similar to Gilbert's. Shaw says that Gilbert is a cynic who accepts 'conventional ideals'. Observing that people do not really live up to their ideals, Gilbert makes a mockery of life. Gilbert's position is similar to that of Sergius in *Arms and the Man*. Disillusioned, Sergius 'declares that life is a farce'. Nothing can come of such high ideals, Shaw claims, except cynicism and pessimism. His own plays, however, are not based upon conventional categories of good and evil. He does not consider Sergius odious for falling short of ideals; Sergius is ridiculous because his ideals are impractical. Shaw particularly objects to Archer's claim that Raina's transfer of affection from Sergius to Bluntschli is unnatural. Raina, 'after imaginatively living up to an ideal relation with Sergius, and conceiving a sub-conscious dislike for him under the strain', fell 'in love for the first time with Bluntschli'.

Only one reviewer, A.B. Walkley, in *The Speaker* (28 April 1894), understood Shaw's intention. Walkley clearly distinguished between 'Gilbertism and Shawism'. Gilbert accepts 'current ideals of life and conduct' and shows people not living up to them. 'Gilbertism, then, consists in the ironic humour to be got out of the spectacle of a number of people hypocritically pretending, or naively failing' to live up to conventional ideals. Shaw, however, holds that conventional morality is not valid and the ideals are false. 'His personages, beginning by accepting them as true, are driven by experience to perceive that they are not, that the world won't fit them, and that life cannot be fully and freely lived until they are discarded.' The ironic humour of Shaw's plays comes from 'the spectacle of a number of people trying to apply the current ideals only to find in the end that they won't work'.

Shaw's reply to his critics

In 'A Dramatic Realist to His Critics' (*The New Review*, July 1894, Vol. XI, No. 7) Shaw wrote of Raina:

> in the play of mine which is most in evidence in London just now, the heroine has been classified by critics as a minx, a liar, and a *poseuse*. I have nothing to do with that: the only moral question for me is, does she do good or harm? If you admit that she does good, that she generously saves a man's life and wisely extricates herself from a false position with another man, then you may classify her as you please— brave, generous, and affectionate; or artful, dangerous, faithless— it is all one to me.

The contrast between Bulgaria and Switzerland is part of the comedy. Of the Bulgarians, Shaw says:

> their attempts at Western civilization were much the same as their attempts at war—instinctive, romantic, ignorant. They were a nation of plucky beginners in every department. Into their country comes, in the play, a professional officer from the high democratic civiliz- ation of Switzerland—a man completely acquainted by long, prac- tical experience with the realities of war. The comedy arises, of course, from the collision of the knowledge of the Swiss with the illusions of the Bulgarians.

Shaw says that Sergius is 'an idealist who is made a pessimist by the shattering of his illusions'. Rather than being a cynic, Shaw respects life as it is actually lived:

> I declare that I am tired to utter disgust of imaginary life, imaginary law, imaginary ethics, science, peace, war, love, virtue, villainy, and imaginary everything else, both on the stage and off it. I demand respect, interest, affection for human nature as it is and life as we must still live it even when we have bettered it and ourselves to the utmost.

A new morality

The late-nineteenth century was in intellectual and emotional revolt against the conventions and pieties of the Victorian age. It was an era of such new literary, intellectual and social fashions as the New Woman and the New Drama. Shaw's natural morality should be seen as arising out of the period's intellectual commitment to reshape society with complete rationality, honesty and freedom of thought. Other writers tell us to pursue high ideals or they justify radically new behaviour by affirming new moral systems. Shaw is one of the few writers who tell us that it is sensible and right to do what feels best and what is most useful. He has no preconceived concepts of what is good or bad behaviour. He never says this or that is always right. Natural ethics are concerned with the utility of behaviour in a specific situation. Whatever improves our life is good; whatever makes life more uncomfortable is bad. A lie is good if it saves a life; a lie is bad if it hurts someone. Shaw assumes that any rational, logical behaviour, freed of social myths, will result in social good. In 'A Dramatic Realist to his Critics' he says:

> It does not concern me that, according to certain ethical systems, all human beings fall into classes labelled liar, coward, thief, and so on. I am myself, according to these systems, a liar, a coward, a thief and a sensualist; and it is my deliberate, cheerful, and entirely self-respecting intention to continue to the end of my life deceiving people, avoiding danger, making my bargains with publishers and managers on principles of supply and demand instead of abstract justice, and indulging all my appetites, whenever circumstances commend such actions to my judgment.

Although *Arms and the Man* is a delightful comedy, its purpose is to make us think, by illustrating how people can ruin their lives through false ideals. Thus Raina acts rationally by lying to save Bluntschli, although the telling of lies is frowned upon by society. Louka acts rationally in trying to better herself by winning and then marrying Raina's fiancé. Major Petkoff acts rationally in asking whether Bluntschli can support Raina in the manner to which she is accustomed. Sergius, however, acts irrationally in expecting Raina not to look at another man, in despising himself for being attracted to other women, and in marrying Louka because of a pledge he made to her during a moment of excitement. Sergius also acts irrationally in bravely leading his cavalry against the Serbian machine-guns; it was only luck that prevented the massacre of his regiment by modern weapons. The behaviour of Captain Bluntschli and the play's conclusion insinuate the need for common-sense realism in our expectations and behaviour.

The Fabian Society and *Arms and the Man*

The controversies among the socialists of the period form part of the English context of the writing of *Arms and the Man*. The commonsensical 'hero' of the play, Captain Bluntschli, has characteristics in common with Sidney Webb, the leader of the Fabians. Webb was an undistinguished-looking man who believed in hard work, efficiency, and gradual reform through parliamentary politics. Sergius Saranoff, the romantic nobleman, is partly modelled on R.B. Cunninghame Graham, a handsome Tory radical nobleman who wanted immediate revolutionary change and took direct part in demonstrations. Sergius's oft-repeated remark—'I never withdraw'—alludes to a similar statement made by Graham during a debate in Parliament.

Shaw's reason for making use of characteristics of the two men in his play is to contrast the gradual, middle-class, democratic revolution with Tory, aristocratic revolt.

Aristocratic behaviour

During the nineteenth century the aristocrats, threatened by the growth of industrialism and the middle class, looked to the chivalric behaviour of the past as an ideal in contrast to modern rationalism and efficiency. The conservative reaction is exemplified in the novels of Sir Walter Scott where an older social order is shown to act with great nobility of behaviour. In Scott's *The Heart of Midlothian*, a woman refuses to lie even to save the life of her sister. (Raina has such models in mind when she claims she never lies.)

In the middle of the century the romanticisation of chivalric ideals finds expression in 'The Charge of the Light Brigade', a poem by Lord Tennyson (1809–92), which praises British cavalrymen who, during the Crimean War (1854), were destroyed while charging entrenched Russian artillery. Although the assault was the result of mistaken orders, it was seen as an example of high ideals which were otherwise lost in the modern world. In the second stanza Tennyson writes:

> 'Forward, the Light Brigade!'
> Was there a man dismay'd?
> Not tho' the soldier knew
>   Some one had blunder'd.
> Theirs not to make reply,
> Theirs not to reason why,
> Theirs but to do and die.
> Into the valley of Death
>   Rode the six hundred.

Sergius's suicidal cavalry charge has similarities to the charge of the Light Brigade.

Middle-class socialism

Many of the nineteenth-century aristocracy, such as Byron and Shelley, saw themselves as revolutionaries preaching an equality of spirit, in contrast to the hypocrisy and calculation which they felt were part of the new middle classes. Sergius's marriage with Louka provides an example of aristocratic idealism uniting itself with the brave spirits among the peasantry.

Shaw, however, felt that the aristocracy was no longer a useful social class. Aristocratic notions of bravery, honour, gallantry, and honesty had no role in modern bourgeois society. Aristocratic revolutionaries were romantics more interested in bravery and dramatic posturing than in social reform. Such irrational idealism was a hindrance to the progress of mankind towards an efficient, rational, socialist society. Even the fact that Sergius leads the cavalry and that Bluntschli's soldiers use machine-guns indicates the difference between the former's feudal and the latter's modern attitudes.

If the aim of society should be to improve the life of all men and promote social justice, then the agent for change is the middle class, which is efficient, practical, rational, and democratic. Being realistic, the middle class is capable of an unbiased view of the uselessness of most social and moral conventions. One function of drama is to educate the middle class to its new role by making it see clearly that the issues involved in most conflicts are between outmoded, useless ideals and natural, useful behaviour which will produce social good.

Shaw's notion of socialism is thus radically different from usually accepted notions. He sees the middle class, as represented by Bluntschli and Switzerland in *Arms and the Man*, as the revolutionary element which will transform society.

Shaw did not believe in a revolutionary working class. The working class of his time was largely subservient to the rich and respectful to them. In *Arms and the Man* Shaw implies that poverty has made Nicola act humbly and respectfully towards the wealthy and influential. Nicola illustrates the conservatism of the working class by being proud of his status as a Petkoff servant. Being afraid of losing his job and returning to the poverty of past generations, he cannot afford to offend others; therefore, he uses his intelligence to find backing to open a shop. He is a part of the poor who are as much involved in capitalism as the rich. Louka, however, is in a mood of revolt at being a servant. She feels the indignity of being in an inferior social position. Her success in trapping Sergius into marriage shows that those who refuse to accept the conventions of society may get what they want, especially if they make use of the idealism of others.

The New Woman

The New Women wanted to be freed from such stereotypes as dependency and weakness; they wanted equality with men. *Arms and the Man* reflects this climate of intellectual opinion. Raina claims to be braver than Bluntschli; Louka taunts Sergius by saying that she has more courage than he has. Raina is shown to have more spirit and vitality than Sergius. She does the one truly brave act in the play by saving Bluntschli. Both Louka and Raina may be said to pursue their future mates actively, whereas the men appear passive and unaware that the women have designs on them.

Each of the women is a strong character. Louka and Raina have energy and realistically seek their goals without paying attention to conventional morals beyond making a false public impression to deceive others. Even Catherine is domineering, cunning, and has few scruples. Shaw obviously likes this quality of common sense in women and sees them as in many ways stronger than men.

Shaw does not idealise women. The women in *Arms and the Man* lie, spy, eavesdrop, provoke quarrels, and use any means available to succeed. If Shaw shows women as equal to men he also strips them of the protection in which society has usually shrouded and idealised the female sex. For Shaw sexual equality includes the emancipation of men from conventional protective attitudes towards women. Bluntschli, for example, is rude to Raina when he accuses her of continually lying. He also is aware throughout the play that Catherine uses lies to gain what she wants. Shaw does not condemn such behaviour in women; he even seems to admire it as showing vitality and life. He does, however, create laughter by revealing the discrepancy between how women pretend to feel and how they actually behave.

Ideas and passions

It is sometimes said that Shaw's characters are too simple and lack depth. This is not exactly true. The characters are seldom shown in any depth, but their complexities are briefly indicated, perhaps too briefly in some cases, and the subsequent action follows from hints previously given. We early suspect Raina's attraction towards Bluntschli, her growing dislike of Sergius, Louka's rivalry with Raina, and Bluntschli's failure to comprehend Raina's actions.

A criticism related to Shaw's supposed lack of ability to show depth of character is his supposed lack of interest in his characters' emotional life. According to some critics Shaw is exclusively concerned with ideas.

While Shaw is more concerned with ideas than passions, it is not true that he ignores passions. It would be more correct to say that Shaw lightly or deftly suggests his characters' emotions without explaining them in detail. We are aware, for example, of Raina's lack of sexual interest in Sergius by the way she holds his portrait in Act I. We feel Raina's sexual interest in Bluntschli although this is never stated. In a sense the battle of personalities between Raina and Bluntschli is a kind of courtship. Raina would not go through rapidly changing moods of disdain, generosity, pride, and interest if she did not feel attracted towards the blood-splattered, filthy, tired soldier. Louka recognises this immediately. She assumes there is no other explanation for Raina's behaviour in hiding the soldier.

Love and romantic ideals

It is too often assumed that *Arms and the Man* is solely a satire on romantic love and aristocratic ideas of warfare. According to such a view Shaw's play is limited to a demonstration of the utility of rational behaviour. But if this is so, why does Raina save Bluntschli, why does Bluntschli return to the Petkoff house, why are we impressed by Louka's bravery and defiance? Certainly there is romance and bravery enough in the play, although it is not where we expect to find it. Shaw is not criticising love, impulse, generosity, or bravery; he is showing the foolishness of acting by false systems of behaviour which mislead us in our attitudes towards love and bravery.

The most impulsively romantic and brave act in the play is Raina's hiding of Bluntschli in Act I. It is both a generous deed which helps others and is founded upon her growing interest in this, to her, strange soldier. The action is radically different from Sergius's suicidal cavalry charge at the Serbian machine-gunners. Sergius is needlessly acting a part; Raina acts nobly in a situation thrust upon her. She also acts warmly when she puts her portrait in the coat she gives the Swiss. By way of contrast, Sergius shows no real passion in the play. His love of Raina is talk. He attempts to flirt with Louka and is surprised to find her a real person with feelings and emotions.

That pure efficiency and reason are not enough to make sense of life is shown by Bluntschli's complete failure to see that Raina is seriously attracted to him. Even Sergius can see what Bluntschli does not suspect until Raina calls him an idiot who is unable to tell the difference between a girl and a woman. *Arms and the Man* puts a premium on romance, love, and bravery, although it distinguishes between their reality and false, idealistic notions learned from books and opera.

Shaw's sense of the theatre

Shaw was both a professional drama critic and a professional director, who often produced his own plays. Surviving scripts of productions that he directed show his detailed supervision of the scenery and the objects on stage, and the guidance he gave his actors. Shaw insisted that a director should have the details of a performance in his head before beginning rehearsals. The director should 'block out' (prepare a plan for) the movements of the actors on stage in advance.

The text of *Arms and the Man* shows Shaw's stagecraft. Although the script we have gives less directions and information than we might expect in a rehearsal script, it is surprisingly detailed and reveals the theatrical quality of Shaw's play.

The first characteristic of Shaw's text to be noticed is the fullness of the descriptions he gives of the scenery and characters. For instance, the opening description in Act I not only tells us about the occupants of the Petkoff house, but also gives us a clear picture of the stage. Shaw has planned the stage so that the various events in the text will work effectively in performance. Throughout the play we are given detailed information about how and where the characters are to move. (Observe Shaw's directions written in square brackets. It would be a useful exercise to draw on paper a plan of the stage and, by using pins, to trace the movements of the characters.) Each furnishing or object is carefully placed so that it will be visible to the audience. As Raina is influenced by her reading of literature, and is proud of the small family library, Shaw's stage directions include a 'pile of paper-backed novels' on the chest of drawers near the bed.

Shaw's sense of what makes good theatre can be seen from the dramatic entrance of Bluntschli into Raina's room. Shaw takes what is a common situation in drama and, by careful attention to details and timing, gives it a new vitality. First Raina hears shots and blows out the candle, leaving her room dark except for the 'starlight seen through the slits at the top of the shutters'. There is distant gun-fire; then several shots near the house. While the shots can still be heard the shutters are pulled open from outside. For an instant we see the window space filled with starlight, the silhouette of a man, and then, immediately, the shutters close. The room is once more dark. We hear a voice panting, we hear the sound of something being scratched and see the flare of a match. As the match goes out, Raina cries out asking who is there. The room is still black and a man's voice warns her not to shout or she will be shot. We hear her trying to rise from the bed and the voice warns her against trying to escape. He then commands her to light a candle. Now for the first time we see the man. He is a dramatic sight. He has blood and snow on his badly torn clothes. He looks at Raina and says politely but menacingly that he is a fleeing Serbian soldier.

If the unexpected intrusion of a man through the window of a woman's room is a 'stock' situation in drama, only an excellent playwright could have handled the quick building up of the scene with the intensifying dramatic effect Shaw achieves. Notice his use of the shutters, lighting, and the excitement of not identifying the man even after he has entered the room. Excitement is created by the momentary appearance of the silhouette, the panting, the scratching sound, the match, the voice from the dark, and the filthy, tattered uniform.

Another excellent dramatic moment occurs in Act II when Bluntschli arrives at the Petkoff house. Catherine attempts quickly to get rid of him. Major Petkoff rushes in and, in an anti-climax, welcomes Bluntschli instead of being angry. Raina stumbles on Bluntschli's presence, calls him her 'chocolate cream soldier' and quickly makes up an excuse; then Nicola brings Bluntschli's bag with Major Petkoff's coat, and quickly realises he has done wrong and covers up the situation. Tension and humour are mixed; suspense over whether Petkoff will realise that his wife and Raina were the two women in Sergius's story is given comic relief by the blunders of Raina and Nicola.

Other good scenes include Sergius's challenge of Bluntschli to a duel (a situation which ends in an anti-climax when Sergius decides that the Swiss is too cold-blooded to fight), Louka's making Sergius kneel and kiss her hand, and the rapid events which conclude the play, including Bluntschli's striking announcement of his wealth.

We should also notice the touches that Shaw gives his characters. Bluntschli's searching in the chocolate box and licking his fingers, Catherine using the serving tray as a mirror, Louka carrying Bluntschli's calling card in her blouse. While such details add to our sense of the characters, they are also good stagecraft. When Sergius repeatedly folds his arms and declares that he never apologises, the gesture may seem a little artificial for a novel, but on stage, where effects must be obvious, the repetition is extremely striking and increasingly comic.

Part of the effect of *Arms and the Man* results from the use of a small cast of characters and the setting of the scene in one place. Each act takes place in a room of Petkoff's house. Acts II and III take place on the same day. There is thus a concentration of effect corresponding to the focus of the play's action on one family, its servants, and the two men friends of the daughter.

The construction of *Arms and the Man*

Shaw's basic unit of construction is a short scene, usually consisting of an exchange of ideas or opinions between a few characters. Shaw's plots do not flow forward in a single, uninterrupted line. Instead, short scene follows short scene fairly rapidly. With each scene there is a change in the persons on stage. Characters and topics often drop out of sight for long periods of time until Shaw is ready to take them up again. This style of construction allows Shaw to develop several stories (Bluntschli —Raina; Raina—Sergius; Sergius—Louka; Louka—Nicola) during an act and, by emphasising personal relations and discussion, it allows him to show the effect of ideas and opinions on behaviour.

Major Petkoff's coat

The dramatic device of the loan of a coat as a means of linking and developing scenes is based upon a similar situation in Eugène Scribe's play, *Bataille de Dames*. The similarity between the two plays shows that while Shaw reacted against the lack of intellectual significance in the late nineteenth-century well-made play, he used many of its devices for organising his own plays.

The coat is given to Bluntschli by Catherine so he can cover his torn, blood-splattered clothes and escape. Later Major Petkoff and Sergius hear that Bluntschli escaped with the help of a woman and her daughter who gave him the husband's coat. Bluntschli returns to the Petkoff house to see Raina again and brings the coat back in a bag. Major Petkoff has been searching for his coat and is told by Catherine that it is in the closet. He says that he has looked in there for it, but Nicola brings him the coat and says it was in the closet.

Next we learn that Raina put a picture of herself, inscribed to the chocolate cream soldier, in the coat pocket. When she learns that Bluntschli never found the picture, she is anxious to obtain it before the secret of her helping the Swiss to escape is discovered. She persuades her father to remove the coat from his back and she takes the picture out of the pocket. Now she thinks she is safe. But her father has indeed already seen the picture and starts questioning her about it. His questions and the reactions to them lead to the resolution of events when Bluntschli is found to be the chocolate cream soldier. Bluntschli tries to dismiss the incident by saying that Raina is too young to have acted seriously. This infuriates her. She tears up the picture and throws it in his face. This forces him to think about her previous behaviour and leads to his proposing to marry her.

The coat with the picture in its pocket is a clever device to precipitate events in the plot. The incidents involving the coat have no meaning in themselves, but show how well Shaw could make a highly elaborate, laughter-producing plot. Shaw, however, influenced by Ibsen, weaves into his plot dialogue which raises serious issues about moral conduct and life.

The stage directions

Shaw's stage directions are also useful in presenting the characters fully. They fill in what is only implied by the dialogue. At the beginning of Act I we are aware that Raina is more anxious over the safety of her father than that of her fiancé, Sergius. Her mother's fascination with bravery and patriotism is suggested by the eagerness and enthusiasm with which she informs Raina of the victory and her indignation at Raina's confession that she previously distrusted heroic ideals. The stage directions thus offer a further dimension to the characters. We sense something of a tension between Catherine's desire for her daughter to marry Sergius and Raina's own lack of enthusiasm. Moreover, we may feel, although this is not made explicit, that Catherine's wishes on this matter are part of her snobbish desire to climb socially and be a fashionable 'lady'. Earlier Catherine's snobbishness was made clear in the stage direction indicating that she wears 'a fashionable tea gown on all occasions'. Catherine's will power is further shown by such directions as 'authoritatively', 'businesslike', 'she strides', 'vehemently, shaking very hard'.

The play's final scene consists of quick transitions of emotion. These would be particularly difficult to follow outside the theatre without Shaw's stage directions and comments. When Bluntschli says Raina is only seventeen years old, his remark 'produces a marked sensation', but he 'proceeds innocently'. He says 'complacently' to Raina that he has cleared up the misunderstanding about the night in November. She 'tears' up the photograph and 'throws the pieces in his face'. He is first 'overwhelmed', then 'considers' and, 'making up his mind', decides to propose to Raina. She 'mutinously' objects to her parents consenting to the marriage and is 'pretending to sulk'; he must look at her 'face-to-face' before she, 'succumbing with a shy smile', accepts his proposal. The psychology of the characters can be seen in the directions as to how the parts are to be played.

It would be a useful study exercise to draw up a list of Shaw's remarks for each person in the play.

Range of characters

Shaw felt that a play should consist of a variety of types of character to interest the audience and to provide dramatic contrast. In *Arms and the Man* there is a noticeable variety of characters, ranging from the aristocratic romanticism of Sergius to the calculating servility of Nicola. In between, the spectrum of types includes the mixed romantic idealism and vital warmth of Raina, the calm, humorous, common-sense efficiency of Bluntschli, the snobbery and deceitfulness of Catherine, the easy-going nature of Major Petkoff, and the mixture of brave insolence and cunning in Louka. The play provides a social range, a spectrum of recognisable types of character, and a variety of temperaments. Each character has a different personality, different ways of speech and dress, and different attitudes towards a situation.

Raina's protection of Bluntschli from the Bulgarian soldiers is seen by Sergius as deceitful to his love, by Major Petkoff as the kind of clever success he associates with Bluntschli. Catherine sees Raina's actions as threatening to endanger both their reputations and perhaps weaken her dominance over her husband. Louka immediately recognises that Raina is in love with the Swiss. Bluntschli assumes that Raina acts from a schoolgirl's love of adventure. At the end of the play, when Bluntschli asks permission to propose to Raina, Catherine is concerned about his social standing, Major Petkoff is concerned about his financial resources, while Raina objects to their considering such practical matters.

Raina

Raina is perhaps the most interesting character in the play. She goes through more rapid transitions of mood and personality than any of the other characters. In reading her part we need to be aware that there is often a contradiction between what she says and what she feels. She criticises the fleeing Swiss soldier for not being a gentleman while simultaneously being attracted to his pitiful condition. She charges Louka with spying on her although she herself has spied on Louka and Sergius. When she is freed from her engagement to Sergius and has Bluntschli's proposal of marriage, she temporarily rejects him.

Throughout most of the play Raina is a romantic idealist, in love with noble-sounding ideas of heroic behaviour which she has learned from books and opera. Later, we realise that her public displays of haughty dignity are blatant deceptions of others. She, in fact, lies and pretends to emotions and ideals that she does not feel. If she is not romantic (in the sense of truly believing in heroic and noble behaviour), she does, however, act romantically in risking her social position to save the Swiss soldier, in immediately falling in love with him, and in placing her portrait in the pocket of the coat with which she helps him to escape. She is beautiful, vital, and conscious of the discrepancy between what she feels and what she thinks she is supposed to feel. She is also capable of anger, quarrelling, and other forms of unideal behaviour. She pretends to help her father make himself comfortable while she removes her portrait from his coat pocket before, she hopes, he will have had time to discover it. She does this with blatant dishonesty in front of Bluntschli and Sergius. She is often dreamy but when interested in what is going on she becomes energetic and quick-thinking.

Early in the play Raina expresses pity for the fleeing, defeated enemy soldiers; she pretends that by saving Bluntschli she is acting nobly, echoing the noble conduct she has seen in operas. When, however, she gives him her portrait, we realise that in helping the soldier she is not only acting according to romantic ideals, she is also attracted towards him. Although he is undistinguished-looking and has threatened her with a gun, she finds his calm realism an interesting contrast to Sergius's heroic mannerisms; as a foreigner of apparently limited financial means he no doubt appears exotic, different, and a man of experience, in contrast to the wealth, provinciality, and protection she has known. She is used to being obeyed and believed. He threatens her and does not believe in her noble talk. It is his difference of outlook on life which attracts Raina as much as his pitiful condition when he is escaping.

When she learns that Bluntschli has told a friend about his adventure in escaping, and when he tells her he has pawned her father's coat as a means of keeping it safe, Raina is angry at his lack of refined feelings. Behind her arrogance is a wish that he would respond romantically towards her, and show his love by romantic behaviour. She is thus both attracted to him because he is different from the false romanticism of Sergius, and she is irritated by the lack of respectful courtesy that she expects from a man. The characteristics which attract her to Bluntschli also annoy her. It is this tension which makes the relationship between Raina and Bluntschli similar to a battle between the sexes. Bluntschli will not accept her haughty posturing and reduces her to an equal when he remarks that he does not believe a single word she says. This is the turning point of the play. From that point onward Raina realises that Bluntschli takes her seriously and she need not try to impress him with her worth as a human being.

Bluntschli

Captain Bluntschli is close to being Shaw's spokesman in the play. He is apparently a cool, efficient realist, with no romantic illusions. Bluntschli first appears in the play as a fleeing soldier who seeks refuge in Raina's bedroom. His concern for his survival leads him to behave in an ungentlemanly fashion to a degree which, while realistic in an escaping soldier, shocks readers brought up on the gallant behaviour of literary heroes. (This is, of course, Shaw's point. A real soldier would act similarly in the circumstances.) He refuses to allow Raina to cover her thin nightgown with a cloak as he knows that her half-dressed state is his best protection against her calling for aid from the wild, drunken, victorious Bulgarian soldiers.

When, however, he thinks the Bulgarian soldiers will discover him, and it is no longer useful to terrorise Raina, he acts decently towards her. After she helps him to avoid discovery, he reveals that he is a professional soldier of fourteen years' experience with no illusions about noble conduct under fire, about brave heroic deeds, or about other ideals that civilians may have about soldiering. He laughs at Sergius's 'heroic' cavalry charge, and admits that he carries chocolates as rations in place of bullets. He quickly gobbles up some chocolates which Raina offers him, searching the box for more and licking the remains from his fingers, and thus becomes Raina's 'chocolate cream soldier', a pitiful, realistic creature, the opposite of the heroic warrior of her imagination.

The next we hear of him is that during the peace negotiations he craftily talked Major Petkoff into accepting two hundred aging horses in exchange for fifty prisoners. Petkoff and Sergius have also heard a story about him escaping in a Bulgarian soldier's coat with the aid of two women. When Bluntschli appears at the Petkoff house, supposedly to return the coat but, as we later learn, to see Raina again, he understands from Catherine's attempts to get rid of him that his presence is unwelcome to her; but he accepts Major Petkoff's invitation to stay and help to plan the return of the Bulgarian soldiers to their provinces.

In quickly solving the problem of transport and supplies, Bluntschli shows his efficiency, in contrast to the incompetent Major Petkoff and the emotional Sergius. The former obviously respects and likes him; Sergius, however, is annoyed at being commanded by a social inferior who treats military life as a trade. Raina is also irritated by his rude practicality and says that he cannot understand her noble ways. When she claims that she has only lied twice in her life, he tells her she is lying. At first shocked, Raina sees that Bluntschli, unlike others, treats her seriously instead of pretending to believe in her flights of fanciful talk.

Bluntschli is always unemotional. At the end of the play he therefore surprises us by saying that he is a romantic who joined the army instead of taking up his father's business and that his romanticism appears in his having come back to see Raina again. He further surprises those listening to him (although perhaps not the audience, which is similarly deceived) by saying that Raina's behaviour is that of a seventeen-year-old schoolgirl. When Raina calls him an idiot and says that she is a woman of twenty-three, Bluntschli realises that she is in love with him. To convince Major Petkoff that he has the means to support Raina, he lists all that he has recently inherited from his father; the recitation of possessions is magnificently comic, including such hotel furnishings as ten thousand knives, forks, and dessert spoons. Instead of the play ending romantically with kisses and love, Bluntschli, still the efficient realist, looks at his watch and announces that he is going away for two weeks to clear up legal matters concerned with his inheritance. Even Sergius is impressed by this final touch of cold-blooded, rational behaviour. Sergius's 'What a man!' alludes to the play's title.

Shaw is suggesting that such practical, unconventional men as Bluntschli are the heroes of the modern world in contrast to the old-fashioned heroism of the past by which Sergius attempts to live. Bluntschli is also a representative of Switzerland (which is implied to be republican, middle-class, unimaginative, worldly, rational) in contrast to Bulgaria (which is seen as feudal, hierarchical, exotic, romantic, innocent, emotional).

Sergius

Sergius is described at the opening of the play as a hero who led his cavalry in a brave attack upon the Serbians and won a great victory. He is engaged to marry Raina with whom he has shared his talk of heroic, romantic ideals. Soon we learn from the escaping Swiss soldier that the cavalry attack on enemy machine-gunners would have been suicidal if the enemy gunners had not been supplied with the wrong ammunition. The Russian officers agree that it was a suicidal act and refuse to promote Sergius, who then threatens to resign. He sees himself as the last of the aristocrats who acted courageously and followed high ideals regardless of the cost, in contrast to the new, unromantic, efficient middle classes.

Holding ideals which neither others nor he himself can match, Sergius has a strong streak of cynicism in his personality. Not being realistic, he oscillates between extreme idealism and extreme despair. Shaw's stage directions say that Sergius is a type first produced in England during the early part of the nineteenth century when the old order came into conflict with the modern world.

Sergius's allegiance to high ideals and his inability to live up to them lead him to self-deception and falseness. His manners are those of old-fashioned gallantry and he speaks ironically of himself and others. He speaks of love in the highest terms to Raina, but in fact he is physically attracted by her servant, Louka. When Louka accuses him and Raina of cheating each other, he is unable to accept that Raina may be like himself and he hurts Louka's arm.

Led on by her taunts, he claims that he has the courage to marry a social inferior and promises that if he ever touches Louka again he will marry her. During the final resolution of events, Sergius's sense of noble obligation leads him to apologise to Louka; carried away by the noble scene he is making he kisses her hand. Reminding him of his former promises, she claims him as a husband. Because of his sense of honour he cannot break his promise to her.

Although Sergius appears to act foolishly throughout the play, he is not a fool. He is handsome, brave, and somewhat intelligent, but he adheres to a foolish system of behaviour. He has come under the influence of Western European romantic ideals which, being unrealistic, cause him to make melodramatic gestures. He continually refuses to apologise (except on the one occasion to Louka), shows his bravery by claiming that he never withdraws, and has the striking gesture of folding his arms whenever he wants to seem superior. He is the kind of handsome, brave, romantic hero about whom many women dream. Shaw's play suggests that a lively young woman would prefer the hardheaded practicality of Bluntschli to a life of impractical dreaming.

Catherine Petkoff

Catherine is the wife of Major Petkoff and Raina's mother. She is over forty years old, energetic, domineering and attractive. She is a snob determined to pass as sophisticated and wears a fashionable tea gown throughout the play. As part of her aping of fashionable society, she has had an electric bell installed; but she is still a peasant at heart and hangs the laundry on bushes to dry. She is a practical woman who takes care of the house, commands others, and is not taken in by Raina's pretences. She is extremely patriotic and urges her husband not to sign a peace treaty. Although she dominates her husband and lies to him, she is also affectionate. At the end of the play she objects that Bluntschli does not come from a noble family such as the Petkoffs, although in fact the Petkoffs can only trace their pedigree back twenty years.

While the three Petkoffs are socially ambitious, Catherine is clearly the driving force behind their attempt to imitate fashionable Western European ways. She improves the house, tries to persuade Raina to marry the noble Sergius, attempts to have Sergius made a general, and, presumably to avoid a scandal, aids her daughter in helping Bluntschli to escape although she, as an extreme patriot, is unlikely to have much sympathy for him. While she has conventional attitudes towards social standing and marriage, she has no conventional scruples in trying to achieve her aims. Presumably she is Shaw's example of how most women behave.

Major Petkoff

Major Petkoff is a type rather than a rounded character. He has little depth or complexity. Shaw describes him as happy, easily excited, and somewhat rough. He is about fifty years old. His only ambitions concern money and his local social standing. He is glad to be home from the wars. His love of domestic comfort is perhaps best demonstrated by his continual fussing about the coat. Being still a peasant at heart he does not believe in washing more than once a week 'to keep up my position' and prefers shouting for the servants in place of using an electric bell. He mocks Sergius's gallant way of speaking. He is, however, proud of his beautiful daughter, Raina. He admits that he was tricked by a Swiss soldier over the exchange of prisoners, and he thinks of war as a trade like any other. He knows that he is rather incompetent at the trade of soldiering and cannot work out how to transport three regiments of troops back to Philippopolis, the capital of Eastern Rumelia. He therefore is glad when Bluntschli visits the house as he hopes the Swiss will solve the problem. He appears to be easily deceived about the disappearance of his coat and other odd happenings, but at the end of the play he surprises us by having quietly understood what was going on between Raina and Bluntschli. He has guessed that Bluntschli is Raina's chocolate cream soldier. He is happy to consent to Bluntschli marrying Raina; however, he first wants to be certain that Bluntschli can support Raina comfortably. When Bluntschli tells him of his wealth, the Major is awed and asks if Bluntschli is Emperor of Switzerland.

Louka

Louka is an impressive combination of cunning and will power. Although a servant, she early impresses us as someone with energy, defiance, and pride, who will either succeed in raising her position in life or will be dismissed from job after job for disobedience. On her first appearance she is described as handsome, proud, defiant, and insolent. She is afraid of Catherine but rude towards Raina, whose air of superiority annoys her. She has a careless manner and walks with a swagger. When Bluntschli sends his calling card to Catherine in Act II, Louka carries the card in her blouse instead of on the proper tray.

When the Russian officer searches Raina's room Louka is the only one to observe Bluntschli's pistol on the ottoman. Because of her knowledge of Raina's secret, Louka acts increasingly insolently. When Nicola warns her to behave better she accuses him of having the soul of a servant; she says no one will ever force her into such servile attitudes. When Sergius flirts with her she pretends to resist him, but in fact leads him on until she can plant in his mind the suggestion that Raina has been unfaithful. She recognises that Raina will marry Bluntschli if they ever meet again and she uses Sergius's romantic dissatisfaction with himself as a means to trap him into marriage. When he hurts her, she disdains his verbal apology and presents her bruised arm to be kissed as if she were a grand lady. She later wears her sleeve tied up to show her naked arm. Although she covers the bruise with a bracelet, she obviously intends to embarrass Sergius into some kind of gesture that will further entangle him with her.

On her next meeting with Sergius she implies that he is not really brave. If she were a mighty queen she would marry the man she loved even if he were socially beneath her. Sergius, she says, would not dare to act so bravely. She claims he is not good enough to be loved by her. Outraged, Sergius falls into the trap and foolishly declares that if he ever touches her again he will have the courage to marry her.

When Raina mocks Sergius by telling the others he is pursuing their servant girl, Louka sees her opportunity. She angrily turns on Sergius and claims that everyone is insulting her because of him. She demands an apology. She carefully phrases her demand by appealing to Sergius's sense of dignity and pride. He will not, she knows, apologise to an equal, but he cannot object to asking the pardon of a poor servant. Touched by her romantic appeal, he kneels to beg forgiveness. She gives him her hand. When he kisses it she reminds him of his promise to marry her if he again touches her. Again playing upon his romantic sense of honour she offers to let him withdraw his promise, which he, of course, refuses to do. As a final act of defiance she calls Raina by her first name, saying that she has a right to call her Raina since Raina calls her Louka.

Louka is an impressive and fascinating character. We are never clear how much of her behaviour is pure, instinctive bravery and how much is calculated. Indeed her behaviour corresponds to Sergius's own notion of heroism and contempt for the petty cautions of others. After the play was produced Shaw several times wrote that Sergius was a romantic fool to marry her. She does seem a formidable woman to marry!

Nicola

Nicola is described as a middle-aged man, proud of his status as a servant of the Petkoffs. Shaw says that he is a cool, accurate calculator with no illusions about life. Nicola warns Louka that if she quarrels with the Petkoffs he will not marry her, as he needs the family's business when he opens his shop in Sofia. He is conscious of the power and influence of the wealthy. He is also discreet and keeps family secrets. He is cleverer than Louka and manages to trick her into revealing what she knows about Raina and Bluntschli. He is always an extremely competent servant and will even pretend to be incompetent rather than create an embarrassing situation for Catherine Petkoff, whom he recognises as the real master of the house.

When Nicola realises that Louka may have a chance to marry Sergius he gives her advice on how to behave. He calculates that if Louka is married to Sergius and buys from his shop, it will be better for him than if he marries her. Towards the end of the play he pretends he was never engaged to Louka so that she can marry Sergius. Whereas Sergius thinks Nicola's lie is either base or heroic, Bluntschli recognises it as totally practical, and calls Nicola the ablest man he has so far met in Bulgaria.

Shaw's admiration for Nicola's realism is clear. Nicola has no romantic illusions and does whatever will advance him towards obtaining a shop, his aim in life. He does not want to be a poor peasant on a farm and hopes to advance to being a shopkeeper. Presumably he is an example of those workers who Shaw felt would never be revolutionary because their own interests are tied to the middle and wealthy classes.

Russian officer

The Russian officer only appears briefly in Act I. He apparently has aristocratic ideals of behaviour similar to those of Sergius and Raina. He accepts Raina's word that no foreign soldier is in her room, even though Bluntschli's pistol is lying on the ottoman where it would be easily noticeable if the officer had even briefly inspected the room.

Language and character

Differences in personality and point of view are expressed in the styles of speech given to each character. Diction, sentence patterns, and other details of language tell us much about each character; changes in the way a character speaks reveal new moods and opinions.

Sergius speaks in an unnatural, formal, 'literary' style (which probably shows the influence of reading Byron and Pushkin, and attending operas), full of pride, dignity, aristocratic disdain for others, irony, and scorn. When hurt he uses melodramatic expressions.

When we first see Sergius, he uses scrupulously gallant expressions towards Catherine: 'My dear mother, if I may call you so.' He often speaks with grave irony and uses parallelism: 'Madam: it was the cradle and the grave of my military reputation.' His speeches sound as if they were written in advance:

I won the battle the wrong way when our worthy Russian generals were losing it the right way. In short, I upset their plans, and wounded their self-esteem. Two Cossack colonels had their regiments routed on the most correct principles of scientific warfare. Two major-generals got killed strictly according to military etiquette. The two colonels are now major-generals; and I am still a simple major.

In the above example, notice how the speech begins with 'I' and after referring to 'two Cossack colonels' and 'two major-generals' ends with the antithetical contrast 'The two colonels are now major-generals; and I am still a simple major'. Also notice the antithetical, balanced contrast in the first sentence: 'I won . . . the wrong way . . . generals were losing it the right way.' In the second sentence there is the parallelism of 'I upset their plans, and wounded their self-esteem'. 'Upset' is balanced against 'wounded'; 'plans' is balanced against 'self-esteem'. Sergius's liking for balance can be seen in even such simple remarks as 'How is Raina; and where is Raina?'. When Sergius becomes disillusioned by his behaviour, he still speaks rhetorically. Notice the parallel 'what would' and 'if' in each sentence that follows:

What would Sergius, the hero of Slivnitza, say if he saw me now? What would Sergius, the apostle of the higher love, say if he saw me now? What would the half dozen Sergiuses who keep popping in and out of this handsome figure of mine say if they caught us here?

Sergius's speeches are filled with exclamations: 'My lady and my saint!'; 'Devil! devil!'; 'Damnation!'; 'Invaluable man!'; 'Damnation! Oh, damnation! Mockery! mockery everywhere!'. His attempts at humour are also formal, as if he were continually acting on a stage: 'Welcome, our friend the enemy!'. Besides having an image of himself as part chivalric hero, he also sees himself partly as a stage villain. In his angry moods Sergius's speeches sound as if he were a villain in a nineteenth-century melodrama: 'I will kill the Swiss; and afterwards I will do as I please with you'; 'Yes: we shall see. And you shall wait my pleasure'. Sergius seldom contracts 'I will', 'You have', or 'do not' into 'I'll', 'you've', or 'don't', except when he is angry and then his speech becomes quicker. Normally he speaks very precisely and oratorically.

Captain Bluntschli's speech patterns are usually short, simple sentences marked with a touch of humour. He uses ordinary phrases, common idioms, and extreme contractions. His speeches are relaxed, calm, and blunt. His first words in the play are 'Dont call out; or youll be shot'. His expressions are common-place, ready-made figures of speech: 'Be good'; 'no harm will happen to you'; 'Take care'; 'it's no use'; 'A good idea!'; 'I'm done for'; 'Dont mention it'; 'Keep out of the way'; 'it will not be nice'; 'just half a chance'; 'keep your head'; 'devil of a fight'; 'I couldnt believe my eyes'. The only time Bluntschli resorts to striking rhetorical statements is at the end of the play when he wishes to impress the Petkoffs with his wealth so that they will approve his marriage to Raina. He forcefully repeats 'I have' as if it were a blunt weapon being used to break their resistance:

I have. I have nine thousand six hundred pairs of sheets and blankets, with two thousand four hundred eider-down quilts. I have ten thousand knives and forks, and the same quantity of dessert spoons. I have three hundred servants. I have six palatial establishments, besides two livery stables, a tea garden, and a private house. I have four medals for distinguished services; I have the rank of an officer and the standing of a gentleman; and I have three native languages.

The language and style of speech of Raina oscillate between a queenly, haughty manner (similar to Sergius's pomposity) when she is trying to impress, and a direct eagerness when her emotions are revealed. In her dignified, grand mood she is often disdainful: 'Some soldiers, I know, are afraid to die'; 'You dared to laugh!'; 'It is not the weapon of a gentleman!'. In her haughty mood, when she is trying to impress, she speaks in generalisations; she could indeed be a queen speaking in the impersonal plural form for her country:

No: you are one of the Austrians who set the Serbs on to rob us of our national liberty, and who officer their army for them. We hate them!

When being imperial she, like Sergius, uses parallel grammatical forms:

'Do you know, sir, that though I am only a woman, I think I am at heart as brave as you.' She is also exclamatory when idealising: 'Yes, first one! the bravest of the brave!'; 'My hero! My king!'. She impersonalises relationships, making herself sound superior to the person she addresses: 'Give me back the portrait, sir.'

In her impulsive and pitying mood her speech is direct: 'I'll help you. I'll save you'; 'I can. I'll hide you'; 'I'm sorry. I wont scold you'. Notice the contractions in the last speech. When she relaxes she speaks in ready-made, common phrases: 'The little beast!'; 'To go and tell!'; 'I'd cram him with chocolate creams till he couldnt ever speak again!'.

Major Petkoff speaks in short, cheerful sentences. His speech is informal, colloquial, filled with idioms and various grunts, grumbles, 'eh's and 'er's. Again the first speech of the character in the play is indicative of how the character will continue to speak: 'Breakfast out here, eh?'. His speech consists, like Bluntschli's, of ready-made phrases: 'Louka's been looking after me. The war's over'; 'would have kept me too long away from you. I missed you greatly'; 'these modern customs'; 'it's not natural'; 'Look at my father!'; 'I dont mind'; 'I did my best'; 'I'll tell you something Ive learnt too'. Notice that his words are often monosyllabic, and that he uses extreme contractions. Major Petkoff's talk seems spontaneous and direct to the point of rudeness: 'Bosh!'; 'Are you deaf?'; 'It's no use'; 'What! that Swiss fellow?'; 'I'll never trust a Swiss again. He humbugged us'. Often his sentences are incomplete: 'You remember. About his being hid by two women'; 'Pooh! nonsense! what does it matter?'; 'Stuff and nonsense'.

Catherine's speeches have a commanding tone; but when she speaks of, or to, Sergius the style becomes elevated. Her description of the battle at the beginning of the play sounds epic: 'A great battle'; 'Sergius is the hero of the hour, the idol of the regiment'; 'the first man to sweep through their guns'; 'our gallant splendid Bulgarians with their swords and eyes flashing, thundering down like an avalanche'.

Style

Although Shaw has a reputation for brilliant repartee, witty paradoxes and the humorous inversion of logic, these are not common to the speeches in *Arms and the Man*. Instead the characters normally use simple, direct, unadorned sentences, based upon colloquial, educated spoken English, except when Raina and Sergius attempt to impress others and use more formal rhetorical expression. The speeches, however, are sometimes tinged with irony or slight satiric barbs: 'our people will be ready for them, you may be sure, now theyre running away'.

Bluntschli's remarks are often comically deflating:

> RAINA *(furious: throwing the words right into his face)* : You have a low shopkeeping mind. You think of things that would never come into a gentleman's head.
>
> BLUNTSCHLI *(phlegmatically)* : Thats the Swiss national character, dear lady.

A stylistic technique that helps to knit the dialogue together is the repetition of a word or figure of speech:

> CATHERINE: Civilized people never shout for their servants. Ive learned that while you were away.
>
> PETKOFF: Well, I'll tell you something Ive learnt too. Civilized people dont hang out their washing to dry where visitors can see it.

The style of the play itself, in contrast to the speeches, is clever, paradoxical, and filled with humorous inversions. The real hero is shown to be the defeated, calculating, unromantic son of a Swiss hotel owner. The usual heroic type, Sergius, is a poor soldier whose bravery is seen as foolish. Romantic love is deflated when Raina chooses the cold-blooded Bluntschli in preference to Sergius, when Sergius is trapped into an engagement with the sharp-tongued servant Louka, and when Nicola denies his engagement to Louka. The reputation of little-visited foreign nations as exotic and romantic is humorously deflated when Bulgaria is shown as striving after Western culture, but so lagging behind that a few books make a library and family titles can only be traced back for twenty years. Shaw does not ridicule others; he creates humour by contrasting impractical ideals with reality.

Other characteristics of Shaw's dramatic style include the use of coincidence, anti-climax, quick transitions in a character's behaviour, the construction of plot around many short scenes, and the use of dialogue instead of action to advance the plot. Further aspects of style have been discussed in the sub-sections: The text of *Arms and the Man*, Shaw's sense of the theatre, The construction of *Arms and the Man*, and Language and character.

Conclusion

Arms and the Man is both an entertaining and a serious play. The characters are lively and sufficiently individualised to be more than 'stock' types. Shaw has a good sense of the theatre, concentrating the play's action into one place and creating effective dramatic situations. He thinks in terms of short, highly effective scenes, many of which end on a humorous anti-climax. The play includes many ironic reversals. Shaw treats romantic situations in a realistic way, revising accepted social ideals and values. His purpose is to show vitality and common sense winning over artificial codes of behaviour. He is not, however, opposed to love or bravery; he is opposed to false notions of love and bravery which trap people into disagreeable roles in life. Shaw wishes to liberate mankind from conventional categories of good and evil. He wants man to live according to what is useful and life-giving instead of what is considered proper or moral. *Arms and the Man* is an effective and agreeably pleasant demonstration of Shaw's philosophy. Its humour arises not from satirising false behaviour but from lifting false illusions.

Part 4

Hints for study

Review questions

(1) The theatrical background to 'Arms and the Man'

(1) Briefly describe the theatre of the 1890s.
(2) Briefly discuss the differences between the plays of Shaw and those of W.S. Gilbert.
(3) What were the basic innovations of Ibsen's plays?
(4) How can the influence of Ibsen be seen in *Plays Unpleasant* and in *Arms and the Man*?
(5) What was the difference between *Plays Unpleasant* and *Plays Pleasant*?
(6) Show how Shaw uses well-made play techniques. Use his treatment of Major Petkoff's coat and Raina's inscribed portrait as your examples.

(2) Shaw's stagecraft in 'Arms and the Man'

(1) Discuss in detail what we learn from the italicised stage settings at the beginning of each act. Write a paragraph on the setting of each act.
(2) Discuss what Shaw's stage directions tell us about *each* character.
(3) Examine in detail the shutter scene (Act I) and at least two other scenes in the play for their theatrical effectiveness. In the case of each scene that you analyse make a detailed description of the progress of events or speeches and explain the dramatic effect. Pay attention to any lighting, sound effects, or other details of performance.
(4) Make a small map of the setting of each act from the italicised stage directions. You should be able to visualise the scene. Trace the movements of the characters on and off stage. Pay particular attention to Act II.
(5) On the basis of stage directions and speeches make a brief description of how each character looks, dresses, gestures, walks and speaks. If you cannot find the information, make a guess which should be supported with a sentence or two explaining the reasons for your guess.
(6) Break down each act into its events. Make an outline of events and state who is on stage during each event.

(7) Write a short essay discussing the use of coincidence in the plot.

(8) Write a short essay on the use of anti-climax.

(9) Show how the first act is similar to a prologue in that it allows Shaw to begin the play in the middle of the story. What advantages are gained by the play's structure of a prologue followed by two concentrated acts?

(3) Themes

(1) Discuss *Arms and the Man* as a satire on foolish ideals about love and war.

(2) Is Shaw's intent to satirise his characters? How does the story show that it is ideals rather than people that are wrong? (In answering this question contrast Raina and Sergius.)

(3) Is Shaw against love and bravery? How does he make a contrast between sincere and insincere behaviour?

(4) Using quotations from Shaw's prose writing and from the play, show how *Arms and the Man* teaches natural ethics.

(5) Show from the play what Bulgaria and Switzerland represent to Shaw.

(6) Discuss the political implications of *Arms and the Man* in relation to Fabianism.

(7) Why is Shaw's hero (Bluntschli) middle class?

(4) Characters

(1) Write a paragraph on each character in the play. Your character sketch should include a description of the character's appearance, personality, habits and what he or she represents.

(2) Shaw's plays are particularly original in the rapid 'transitions' each character undergoes so that we see the character from different perspectives. Make a list of the different ways each character appears or acts during the play. Make clear the contrasts to or transitions from the way the character previously acted or was seen.

Study questions

Act I

(1) What do we learn about Bulgaria in Act I?

(2) Why does Shaw include long stage directions in his plays and what does his opening description of the scene show about Raina and her family?

(3) Discuss the characters of Raina and the Swiss soldier.
(4) Contrast the various descriptions of Sergius.
(5) Discuss the significance of the mentions of opera and literature in Act I.

Act II

(1) Describe Sergius's character, behaviour, and attitudes.
(2) What does Shaw show us about social classes in Bulgaria in Act II?
(3) Discuss the use of anti-climax and coincidence in Acts I and II.
(4) Describe Nicola's character.
(5) Describe how the other characters view Sergius.

Act III

(1) Discuss the use made of Major Petkoff's old coat within the play.
(2) Write a summary of the events and attitudes of the characters from the time Louka is found listening at the door until the final curtain.
(3) Write a character description of Catherine.
(4) Discuss how *Arms and the Man* illustrates Shaw's opinion that instead of man being the pursuer, it is woman who chooses her mate and pursues him.
(5) Discuss Bluntschli as a realist and a romantic.

Illustrative quotations

You should have full understanding of the plot, characters, themes, and structure of the play. You should have quotations available to illustrate your points. It would be a useful exercise to learn suitable quotations to illustrate each of these points. For example, in Act III the turning point of the play occurs with Raina's admission to Bluntschli: 'How did you find me out?'.

Sergius's Byronic contempt for servility and caution is illustrated by his remark 'And if one of them is man enough to spit in my face for insulting him, I'll buy his discharge and give him a pension'. This remark also looks forward to his engagement to Louka as she has gained his respect by standing up to him.

Louka's baiting of Sergius challenges his idea of himself as brave, courageous, and superior to others. The following passage leads into the scene where she claims that she is more brave than he is and therefore superior: 'How easy it is to talk! Men never seem to me to grow up: they all have schoolboy's ideas. You don't know what true courage is.'

Bluntschli's reply to Major Petkoff – 'My rank is the highest known in Switzerland: I am a free citizen' – can be used to show how Shaw sees democracy, middle-class efficiency, and progress as a contrast to feudalism and romantic ideals.

For examination purposes learn four usefully illustrative quotations from each act. Study the significance and the context of the following passages:

Act I

'It proves that all our ideas were real after all.' Raina says this after she hears of Sergius's brave cavalry charge.

'And there was Don Quixote flourishing like a drum major, thinking he'd done the cleverest thing ever known, whereas he ought to be court-martialled for it.' Bluntschli is describing Sergius's cavalry charge. The speech occurs just before the climax of Act I when Raina shows Bluntschli the portrait of 'the patriot and hero – to whom I am betrothed'.

'The poor darling is worn out. Let him sleep.' Raina says this to Catherine at the end of Act I.

'Oh, you are a very poor soldier: a chocolate cream soldier!' Raina exclaims after Bluntschli has said that he cannot face trying to escape down the drainpipe. Notice that Shaw's stage directions say 'she stoops over him almost maternally'.

Act II

'You have the soul of a servant.' Louka says this to Nicola when he has told her to hold her tongue and serve the family faithfully if she wants to make the most out of her place. She says afterwards, 'Youll never put the soul of a servant into me'. Later Sergius insults her by saying she has 'the soul of a servant' when she informs him of Raina's other man.

> *By his brooding on the perpetual failure, not only of others, but of himself, to live up to his ideals; by his consequent cynical scorn for humanity; by his jejune credulity as to the absolute validity of his concepts and the unworthiness of the world in disregarding them; by his wincings and mockeries under the sting of the petty disillusions which every hour spent among men brings to his senstive observa-tion, he has acquired the half tragic, half ironic air, the mysterious moodiness, the suggestion of a strange and terrible history that has left nothing but undying remorse.*

The above is Shaw's description of Sergius on his first entrance. It explains his irony and disillusionment with himself, which is soon shown when Sergius asks himself 'Which of the six is the real man . . . One is . . . like all cowards'.

> I always feel a longing to do or say something dreadful to him – to shock his propriety – to scandalize the five senses out of him. . . . I dont care whether he finds out about the chocolate cream soldier or not. I half hope he may.

Raina says this to Catherine when her mother warns her that Sergius will break the engagement if he finds out about the night in November.

Act III

Identify the context and explain the importance of the following quotations:

> LOUKA: Not to you, his equal and his enemy. To me, his poor servant, he will not refuse to apologize.

> BLUNTSCHLI: What nonsense! I assure you, my dear Major, my dear Madame, the gracious young lady simply saved my life, nothing else. She never cared two straws for me. Why, bless my heart and soul, look at the young lady and look at me. She, rich, young, beautiful, with her imagination full of fairy princes and noble natures and cavalry charges and goodness knows what! And I, a commonplace Swiss soldier who hardly knows what a decent life is after fifteen years of barracks and battles: a vagabond, a man who has spoiled all his chances in life through an incurably romantic disposition, a man –

> CATHERINE: I doubt, sir, whether you quite realize either my daughter's position or that of Major Sergius Saranoff, whose place you propose to take. The Petkoffs and the Saranoffs are known as the richest and most important families in the country. Our position is almost historical: we can go back for twenty years.

> BLUNTSCHLI: I wont take that answer. I appealed to you as a fugitive, a beggar, and a starving man. You accepted me. You gave me your hand to kiss, your bed to sleep in, and your roof to shelter me.

Sample answers

(1) Discuss 'Arms and the Man' as an entertaining play

Shaw's purpose as a dramatist was to entertain and educate. He was aware that the production of a play costs large sums of money and therefore a play must please while it educates the audience. Too often critical attention is paid solely to the meaning of *Arms and the Man* while its entertainment value is neglected. It is, however, an extremely funny play.

The main humour of *Arms and the Man* is related to its themes of bravery and love. In trying to act according to foolish romantic ideals, such characters as Raina and Sergius become humorous. We quietly smile, although we do not laugh, at Sergius when he claims that Bluntschli is his rival for the affections of Raina and challenges him to a duel, although Sergius himself had the moment before attempted to make love to Louka. We also quietly smile at Raina's haughty, dignified airs.

Another more direct form of humour occurs when characters descend from their dignified poses to speak or act what they really feel. In Act II Raina and Sergius speak to each other with extreme intensity about love. As soon as Raina leaves the stage and Louka enters, Sergius says to her that 'higher love' is a 'very fatiguing thing to keep up for any length of time. One feels the need of some relief after it'. In this case, we laugh at the discrepancy between fanciful illusions of how people should behave and the reality of what they feel.

Still another form of humour results from Bluntschli's honest, blunt reactions in contrast to Raina's attempts to act nobly or with dignity. In Act I when Raina learns that Bluntschli's pistol is not loaded and that he carries chocolates instead, she attempts to humiliate him by offering him chocolates. Instead of being humiliated he exclaims 'Creams! Delicious!' and gobbles the chocolates.

Shaw's use of anti-climax is also entertaining. When Raina shows Bluntschli the photograph of 'the patriot and hero' whom she is going to marry, Act I reaches its climax as the two main characters are now on the verge of a serious conflict of attitudes. But immediately the tension is relaxed and the scene becomes comic when Bluntschli protests that he cannot face descending the waterpipe to escape. 'I darent! The very thought of it makes me giddy.'

This example of anti-climax also illustrates Shaw's comic technique of making his characters act the opposite of what we expect. The professional soldier carries chocolates instead of guns, is afraid to escape down a waterpipe, and is the opposite of brave and warlike.

Arms and the Man is also entertaining because of the absurdly comic situations that develop within the plot. It is amusing that Major Petkoff and Sergius have met Bluntschli after the fighting without realising that Raina and Catherine helped him escape, and that Petkoff invites him to stay at his house. Amusing complications develop at the end of Act II when Raina sees Bluntschli and exclaims 'Oh! The chocolate cream soldier!', and when Nicola, on Catherine's previous instructions, brings

Bluntschli's luggage to the garden. The chain of lies concerning Major Petkoff's coat is humorous. Especially funny is the scene where Bluntschli calls Raina a schoolgirl and she calls him an idiot. The unexpected revelation that she is a twenty-three-year-old woman in love with him catches the audience as well as Captain Bluntschli off guard, because we have also been deceived.

Although the characters in *Arms and the Man* often act in amusing ways, they are not comic characters. Shaw does not laugh at his characters or satirise them as individuals. He laughs at their attempts to live by mistaken or foolish ideas. He does not mock his characters as being hypocrites; he sees people as led by false or unrealistic ideals to behave absurdly.

While *Arms and the Man* has a serious theme it is an entertaining play in which comic situations, the portrayal of foolish ideals, and unexpected behaviour are extremely entertaining.

---

(2) What is Shaw's purpose in 'Arms and the Man'?

Shaw believed that society had progressed beyond the stage where notions of good and evil are valid. Conduct should be related to social utility rather than conventional morals. In *Arms and the Man* he shows the foolishness of old-fashioned conventions of conduct and implicitly approves of actions which are socially useful in making people happy.

To show that conduct should be based upon natural ethics, rather than traditional morals, he has his heroine, Raina, save an enemy soldier by lying to others. She hides him in her room overnight, although such conduct would be considered immoral and unpatriotic by many people. Later we learn that Raina has fallen in love with the escaped soldier, although she was engaged to marry an officer in the Bulgarian Army.

Although some contemporary critics accused Shaw of seeing his characters as hypocrites, Shaw claimed that he was laughing at foolish ideas and not at his characters' behaviour. He approves of Raina's generous act in saving the enemy soldier, her wisdom in lying to save his life, her willingness to break her engagement with Sergius and to admit that she has fallen in love with the stranger.

In contrast to Raina's practical and spontaneous behaviour, her fiancé Sergius is bound to useless codes of conduct. He foolishly leads a cavalry charge against machine-gunners, threatens to quit the army when his foolish bravery does not lead to a promotion, speaks of noble love to Raina while trying to seduce her servant, and eventually marries the servant rather than break a promise she extracted from him.

The value Shaw gives to useful behaviour is also shown by the admiration we feel for the male servant, Nicola. Nicola at first seems too servile and calculating to earn our admiration. As the play progresses, however, we see that he is in command of all situations and has correctly judged how to behave if he is to rise from being a servant to owning his own shop. In a magnificently cunning gesture towards the end of the play he denies that he is engaged to marry Louka so that she can marry Sergius and, he hopes, become an important customer at his shop. Although such behaviour runs against our ideals of romantic love, it is extremely practical for someone in his position.

Shaw shows that life cannot be lived by romantic ideals or old-fashioned views of conduct. By freeing herself from noble notions of conduct Raina saves and marries the man she loves. Shaw's aim, however, is not to show love conquering all, since Nicola is also admired for his common sense in giving up his claim to Louka so that he can eventually have his own shop and free himself from being a servant. Shaw's purpose is to show that behaviour must be useful to the situation and not based upon fixed ideas. Sergius, who has fixed notions of conduct, will probably be very unhappy in his marriage to Louka.

---

(3) Discuss 'Byronism' in 'Arms and the Man'

George Gordon, Lord Byron (1788–1824), was an English poet, author of *Childe Harold's Pilgrimage* and *Don Juan*. He was in revolt against the conventional society of the day. He was against hypocrisy and oppression, and he fought for Greek independence.

Early in *Arms and the Man* Raina wonders if the ideals she and Sergius hold are real or whether they are the result of reading Byron and Pushkin. Later when Sergius first appears in the play Shaw gives him Byronic characteristics, *'brooding on the perpetual failure, not only of others, but of himself, to live up to his ideals'*, *'his consequent cynical scorn for humanity'*, *'his wincings and mockeries under the sting of . . . petty disillusions'*, the *'half tragic, half ironic air, the mysterious moodiness'*.

Sergius's Byronism is shown in his contempt for everything to do with caution, prudence, commerce, trade, and the middle classes. He is moody, aristocratic, and has an exaggerated sense of humour. He is similar to Byron in his association with the national resurgence of a Balkan country, his suicidal heroism, his disdain for practical common sense, and in his admiration of those who disobey. He is similar to Byron in his sexual fickleness (shown by his courtship of Louka while he is supposedly engaged to Raina), and in his contempt for his inability to live up to his own ideals. He is similar to Byron in being a confused mixture of various personalities.

Sergius is, like Byron, representative of an aristocracy that was losing its role in society to the middle classes and consequently held commercial values in contempt. It could be argued that unlike Byron, however, Sergius's posturing has little basis in social reality as the Bulgaria of the play is not an aristocratic society undergoing a transformation to industrialism. Sergius's ideals of chivalric and noble behaviour have been acquired second hand through foreign poetry and operas. His Byronism therefore seems imitative, exaggerated, and laughable.

Questions for further study

(1) Discuss Shaw's relationship to the theatre of the 1890s.
(2) Compare and contrast the various characters in *Arms and the Man*.
(3) Discuss Shaw's dramatic technique in *Arms and the Man*.
(4) Is *Arms and the Man* merely a pleasant comedy?
(5) Why should Shaw, a socialist, write *Arms and the Man*?
(6) Discuss Shaw's anti-romanticism in *Arms and the Man*.
(7) Discuss Shaw's creation of acting parts in *Arms and the Man*.
(8) Discuss the significance of the stage directions in *Arms and the Man*.
(9) Discuss the relationship of the title of *Arms and the Man*.
(10) Discuss *Arms and the Man* as a comedy of reversals.
(11) Contrast Bulgaria with what we are told about Switzerland in the play.
(12) Write an appreciation of *Arms and the Man*, discussing the qualities that make it a successful play.
(13) Discuss Shaw's views of women as shown in *Arms and the Man*.
(14) Discuss *Arms and the Man* as a play illustrating the need for a natural morality.

Part 5

Suggestions for further reading

The text

SHAW: *The Bodley Head Bernard Shaw*, collected plays with their prefaces, 7 vols., editorial supervisor, Dan H. Laurence, Bodley Head, London, 1970–4. This is the standard modern edition.

SHAW: *Plays Pleasant*, Penguin Books, Harmondsworth, 1968. A widely available edition that includes *Candida*, *You Never Can Tell*, *The Man of Destiny*.

SHAW: *Arms and the Man*, edited by A.C. Ward, Longmans, London, 1955. Good introduction and notes.

SHAW: *Arms and the Man*, edited by Louis Crompton, Bobbs-Merrill, Indianapolis, 1969. Good introduction and notes.

Other works by Shaw

SHAW: *Complete Plays*, Paul Hamlyn, London, 1965.

SHAW: *Complete Prefaces*, Paul Hamlyn, London, 1965.

SHAW, AND OTHERS: *Fabian Essays,* with an introduction by Asa Briggs, Allen and Unwin, London, 1962.

SHAW: *The Intelligent Woman's Guide to Socialism, Capitalism, Sovietism and Fascism*, Penguin Books, Harmondsworth, 1965.

SHAW: Collected Letters: 1874–1897, edited by Dan H. Laurence, Reinhardt, London, 1965.

Works on Shaw

BENTLEY, ERIC: *Bernard Shaw: 1856–1950*, Methuen, London, 1957. This is an interesting discussion of Shaw's place in modern thought.

CHESTERTON, G.K.: *George Bernard Shaw,* Max Reinhardt, London, 1961; Hill and Wang, New York, 1966. First published in 1909, this is one of the earliest and still an amusing and perceptive book.

DUKORE, BERNARD: *Bernard Shaw, Director*, University of Washington Press, Seattle, 1971.

GIBBS, A.M.: *Shaw*, Oliver and Boyd, Edinburgh, 1965. A useful introduction in the Writers and Critics series.

KAUFMANN, R.J. (ED.): *G.B. Shaw: A Collection of Critical Essays*, Prentice Hall, Englewood Cliffs, New Jersey, 1965. A useful collection of essays in the Twentieth Century Views series.

MORGAN, MARGERY M.: *The Shavian Playground*, Methuen, London, 1972. A comprehensive study of the form and meaning of the plays.

OHMANN, RICHARD: *Shaw: the Style and the Man*, Wesleyan University Press, Middletown, Connecticut, 1962. A stylistic study.

PEARSON, HESKETH: *Bernard Shaw, his life and personality*, Collins, London, 1950. A good biography.

WARD, A.C.: *Bernard Shaw*, Longman, London, 1951. Still a useful introduction.

The author of these notes

BRUCE KING was educated at Columbia University and the University of Leeds. He has taught English in the United States, Canada, England, Scotland, France and Nigeria. From 1979 to 1983 he was Professor of English at the University of Canterbury, New Zealand, and then Albert Johnston Professor of Literature at the University of North Alabama, spending most of 1984 at the University of Kerala, India. His publications include *Dryden's Major Plays*, *Marvell's Allegorical Poetry*, and *New English Literatures*. He is also the author of York Notes on Ibsen's *A Doll's House* and Fielding's *Joseph Andrews*.

The first 250 titles

<table>
<thead>
<tr><th></th><th>Series number</th></tr>
</thead>
<tbody>
<tr><td>CHINUA ACHEBE</td><td></td></tr>
<tr><td>A Man of the People</td><td>(116)</td></tr>
<tr><td>Arrow of God</td><td>(92)</td></tr>
<tr><td>Things Fall Apart</td><td>(96)</td></tr>
<tr><td>ELECHI AMADI</td><td></td></tr>
<tr><td>The Concubine</td><td>(139)</td></tr>
<tr><td>ANONYMOUS</td><td></td></tr>
<tr><td>Beowulf</td><td>(225)</td></tr>
<tr><td>JOHN ARDEN</td><td></td></tr>
<tr><td>Serjeant Musgrave's Dance</td><td>(159)</td></tr>
<tr><td>AYI KWEI ARMAH</td><td></td></tr>
<tr><td>The Beautyful Ones Are Not Yet Born</td><td>(154)</td></tr>
<tr><td>JANE AUSTEN</td><td></td></tr>
<tr><td>Emma</td><td>(142)</td></tr>
<tr><td>Mansfield Park</td><td>(216)</td></tr>
<tr><td>Northanger Abbey</td><td>(1)</td></tr>
<tr><td>Persuasion</td><td>(69)</td></tr>
<tr><td>Pride and Prejudice</td><td>(62)</td></tr>
<tr><td>Sense and Sensibility</td><td>(91)</td></tr>
<tr><td>HONORÉ DE BALZAC</td><td></td></tr>
<tr><td>Le Père Goriot</td><td>(218)</td></tr>
<tr><td>SAMUEL BECKETT</td><td></td></tr>
<tr><td>Waiting for Godot</td><td>(115)</td></tr>
<tr><td>SAUL BELLOW</td><td></td></tr>
<tr><td>Henderson, The Rain King</td><td>(146)</td></tr>
<tr><td>ARNOLD BENNETT</td><td></td></tr>
<tr><td>Anna of the Five Towns</td><td>(144)</td></tr>
<tr><td>WILLIAM BLAKE</td><td></td></tr>
<tr><td>Songs of Innocence, Songs of Experience</td><td>(173)</td></tr>
<tr><td>ROBERT BOLT</td><td></td></tr>
<tr><td>A Man For All Seasons</td><td>(51)</td></tr>
<tr><td>ANNE BRONTË</td><td></td></tr>
<tr><td>The Tenant of Wildfell Hall</td><td>(238)</td></tr>
<tr><td>CHARLOTTE BRONTË</td><td></td></tr>
<tr><td>Jane Eyre</td><td>(21)</td></tr>
<tr><td>EMILY BRONTË</td><td></td></tr>
<tr><td>Wuthering Heights</td><td>(43)</td></tr>
<tr><td>ROBERT BROWNING</td><td></td></tr>
<tr><td>Men and Women</td><td>(226)</td></tr>
<tr><td>JOHN BUCHAN</td><td></td></tr>
<tr><td>The Thirty-Nine Steps</td><td>(89)</td></tr>
<tr><td>JOHN BUNYAN</td><td></td></tr>
<tr><td>The Pilgrim's Progress</td><td>(231)</td></tr>
<tr><td>GEORGE GORDON, LORD BYRON</td><td></td></tr>
<tr><td>Selected Poems</td><td>(244)</td></tr>
<tr><td>ALBERT CAMUS</td><td></td></tr>
<tr><td>L'Etranger (The Outsider)</td><td>(46)</td></tr>
<tr><td>GEOFFREY CHAUCER</td><td></td></tr>
<tr><td>Prologue to the Canterbury Tales</td><td>(30)</td></tr>
<tr><td>The Franklin's Tale</td><td>(78)</td></tr>
<tr><td>The Knight's Tale</td><td>(97)</td></tr>
<tr><td>The Merchant's Tale</td><td>(193)</td></tr>
<tr><td>The Miller's Tale</td><td>(192)</td></tr>
<tr><td>The Nun's Priest's Tale</td><td>(16)</td></tr>
<tr><td>The Pardoner's Tale</td><td>(50)</td></tr>
<tr><td>The Wife of Bath's Tale</td><td>(109)</td></tr>
<tr><td>Troilus and Criseyde</td><td>(198)</td></tr>
</tbody>
</table>

<table>
<thead>
<tr><th></th><th>Series number</th></tr>
</thead>
<tbody>
<tr><td>ANTON CHEKHOV</td><td></td></tr>
<tr><td>The Cherry Orchard</td><td>(204)</td></tr>
<tr><td>SAMUEL TAYLOR COLERIDGE</td><td></td></tr>
<tr><td>Selected Poems</td><td>(165)</td></tr>
<tr><td>WILKIE COLLINS</td><td></td></tr>
<tr><td>The Moonstone</td><td>(217)</td></tr>
<tr><td>The Woman in White</td><td>(182)</td></tr>
<tr><td>SIR ARTHUR CONAN DOYLE</td><td></td></tr>
<tr><td>The Hound of the Baskervilles</td><td>(53)</td></tr>
<tr><td>WILLIAM CONGREVE</td><td></td></tr>
<tr><td>The Way of the World</td><td>(207)</td></tr>
<tr><td>JOSEPH CONRAD</td><td></td></tr>
<tr><td>Heart of Darkness</td><td>(152)</td></tr>
<tr><td>Lord Jim</td><td>(150)</td></tr>
<tr><td>Nostromo</td><td>(68)</td></tr>
<tr><td>The Secret Agent</td><td>(138)</td></tr>
<tr><td>Youth and Typhoon</td><td>(100)</td></tr>
<tr><td>BRUCE DAWE</td><td></td></tr>
<tr><td>Selected Poems</td><td>(219)</td></tr>
<tr><td>DANIEL DEFOE</td><td></td></tr>
<tr><td>A Journal of the Plague Year</td><td>(227)</td></tr>
<tr><td>Moll Flanders</td><td>(153)</td></tr>
<tr><td>Robinson Crusoe</td><td>(28)</td></tr>
<tr><td>CHARLES DICKENS</td><td></td></tr>
<tr><td>A Tale of Two Cities</td><td>(70)</td></tr>
<tr><td>Bleak House</td><td>(183)</td></tr>
<tr><td>David Copperfield</td><td>(9)</td></tr>
<tr><td>Great Expectations</td><td>(66)</td></tr>
<tr><td>Hard Times</td><td>(203)</td></tr>
<tr><td>Little Dorrit</td><td>(246)</td></tr>
<tr><td>Nicholas Nickleby</td><td>(161)</td></tr>
<tr><td>Oliver Twist</td><td>(101)</td></tr>
<tr><td>Our Mutual Friend</td><td>(228)</td></tr>
<tr><td>The Pickwick Papers</td><td>(110)</td></tr>
<tr><td>EMILY DICKINSON</td><td></td></tr>
<tr><td>Selected Poems</td><td>(229)</td></tr>
<tr><td>JOHN DONNE</td><td></td></tr>
<tr><td>Selected Poems</td><td>(199)</td></tr>
<tr><td>THEODORE DREISER</td><td></td></tr>
<tr><td>Sister Carrie</td><td>(179)</td></tr>
<tr><td>GEORGE ELIOT</td><td></td></tr>
<tr><td>Adam Bede</td><td>(14)</td></tr>
<tr><td>Silas Marner</td><td>(98)</td></tr>
<tr><td>The Mill on the Floss</td><td>(29)</td></tr>
<tr><td>T. S. ELIOT</td><td></td></tr>
<tr><td>Four Quartets</td><td>(167)</td></tr>
<tr><td>Murder in the Cathedral</td><td>(149)</td></tr>
<tr><td>Selected Poems</td><td>(155)</td></tr>
<tr><td>The Waste Land</td><td>(45)</td></tr>
<tr><td>GEORGE FARQUHAR</td><td></td></tr>
<tr><td>The Beaux Stratagem</td><td>(208)</td></tr>
<tr><td>WILLIAM FAULKNER</td><td></td></tr>
<tr><td>Absalom, Absalom!</td><td>(124)</td></tr>
<tr><td>As I Lay Dying</td><td>(44)</td></tr>
<tr><td>Go Down, Moses</td><td>(163)</td></tr>
<tr><td>The Sound and the Fury</td><td>(136)</td></tr>
<tr><td>HENRY FIELDING</td><td></td></tr>
<tr><td>Joseph Andrews</td><td>(105)</td></tr>
<tr><td>Tom Jones</td><td>(113)</td></tr>
</tbody>
</table>

The first ten titles

YORK HANDBOOKS form a companion series to York Notes and are designed to meet the wider needs of students of English and related fields. Each volume is a compact study of a given subject area, written by an authority with experience in communicating the essential ideas to students of all levels.

AN INTRODUCTORY GUIDE TO ENGLISH LITERATURE
by MARTIN STEPHEN

PREPARING FOR EXAMINATIONS IN ENGLISH LITERATURE
by NEIL McEWAN

AN INTRODUCTION TO LITERARY CRITICISM
by RICHARD DUTTON

THE ENGLISH NOVEL
by IAN MILLIGAN

ENGLISH POETRY
by CLIVE T. PROBYN

STUDYING CHAUCER
by ELISABETH BREWER

STUDYING SHAKESPEARE
by MARTIN STEPHEN *and* PHILIP FRANKS

ENGLISH USAGE
by COLIN G. HEY

A DICTIONARY OF LITERARY TERMS
by MARTIN GRAY

READING THE SCREEN
An Introduction to Film Studies
by JOHN IZOD